THE MIDI COMPANION

by JEFFREY RONA

Edited by RONNY S. SCHIFF

Associate Editor SCOTT R. WILKINSON

Graphic Design, Illustrations and Diagrams by WEST DESKTOP GRAPHICS

Cover Graphic by LACHLAN WESTFALL and JEFFREY RONA

Library of Congress Cataloging-in-Publication Data
Rona, Jeffrey C. (Jeffrey Carl), 1957-
The MIDI Companion (formerly: MIDI, the Ins, Outs and Thrus)
1. MIDI (Standard) 2. Computer sound processng.
I. Schiff, Ronny. II. Title. III. The MIDI Companion
MT723.R66 1987   789.9'9   86-27746
ISBN 0-88188-560-6
1994   ISBN 0-7935-3077-6

HAL•LEONARD™
CORPORATION

7777 W. BLUEMOUND RD. P.O. BOX 13819 MILWAUKEE, WI 53213

Table of Contents

Foreword

Hmm, another new book on MIDI? In the first decade of the Musical Instrument Digital Interface, there have been a tremendous number of tomes published on the subject. Some were about as exciting as excerpts from the phone book, focusing too much on the technical, propeller-head stuff—least significant bytes, sys-ex packets, microsecond flurblblobs, and the like, and not enough on the important part of what MIDI actually *does*. It would seem that the authors of some of those lexicons forgot that MIDI is *used by musicians* to make music.

Jeff Rona, whose involvement with MIDI goes back to its introduction, details the technical side of MIDI in all its code crunching glory, but he does it in a way that puts things in musical perspective. It's an approach that should help you to connect the technological dots with an un-intimidating and user-friendly experience, even for the technophobic music-minded MIDI neophytes among you.

Enjoy,

Dominic Milano
Editor
Keyboard Magazine

1

Beginnings

The way music is made has been changed forever. MIDI instruments are now the tools of artists from an enormous range of styles and traditions. The quality, and perhaps even the quantity, of music has grown as a result of the MIDI phenomenon. First, a little history:

The 'sixties and 'seventies were an explosive time for the creation of new musical instruments. In addition to the blossoming use of electric guitars and new keyboards such as electric organs and pianos, a whole new breed of musical instrument was beginning to appear on albums and in concerts—the electronic synthesizer. These large, odd looking and odder sounding machines were based on simple *analog* electronics. They used electrical voltages to create and control sounds. Higher voltages would make higher notes and lower voltages made lower notes. Several small companies began to make instruments, all based on the concept of control voltage (CV). Short electrical cables called *patch chords* would feed the control voltages around these instruments to manipulate the sound's character and shape.

For musicians who wanted to play from a standard organ-like keyboard, special CV keyboards were built to control the rest of the instrument. These early synthesizers could play only a single note (*monophonic*) at a time. To get more musical lines, you either had to buy more synthesizers, or record parts onto tape. These synthesizers were difficult to set up, use and maintain, but they gave those musicians something they could get no other way—fresh new sounds.

The *monophonic* (single note) Moog and ARP brands of synthesizers were already bending quite a few ears by the mid 'seventies with bands such as ELP, Genesis and others, when the Oberheim company introduced the first commercial *polyphonic* (able to play several notes at a time) keyboard synthesizer. Relative to its unwieldy predecessors, it was simple to use, had a built-in keyboard, was able to play four notes at a time (a 400% improvement!), and had a simple array of knobs and switches you could manipulate to quickly create rich, wonderful new sounds. It was far more portable and easy to program than most of its predecessors.

Soon after, more easy to use, good-sounding, polyphonic synthesizers began to appear: Sequential Circuits, Yamaha, Moog, Roland, ARP and other companies introduced new models of electronic instruments, all able to play multiple notes simultaneously. Just a few years earlier, what was an expensive, unwieldy and difficult to use machine, was becoming a popular instrument with a growing crowd of diverse musicians.

After polyphony, perhaps the next most important advance in early synthesizer technology was the incorporation of programmable *memory* into instruments. All polyphonic synthesizers have a small built-in computer that "looks" at each key on the keyboard to see if it has been pressed, and then passes those notes on to the available *oscillators* (which are the special electronic circuits in a synthesizer that make the actual sounds). That small computer could also help store and recall sounds created by the user into the synthesizer's built-in memory (like taking a snapshot of all the knobs and buttons on the instrument). This opened up a whole new world for live performance.

Prior to programmable memory, the reason that people like Keith Emerson and Rick Wakeman had such extravagant keyboard setups on stage was that each of the instruments could only be set-up to produce a single sound per show. Hours of preparation were needed to *patch* together the sounds and the different instruments. When memory came along, it allowed a single synthesizer to be used for several different sounds during a live show or recording session, by simply pressing a single button.

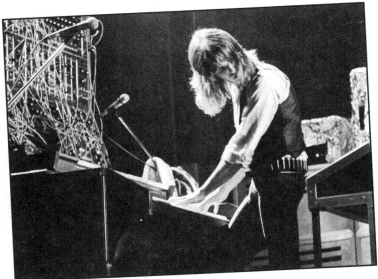

Figure 1-1 Keith Emerson

Adding memory to the synthesizer made it many times more useful. But many early synthesizers—like many cars—had personalities of their own. Some got wonderful, thick brass. Others were more adept at woodwinds, or strings, or bells, or sound effects, or pianos, or colorful tropical birds, or the laugh of small friendly aliens. What was needed next was a way to combine the best of each instrument into a single, useful musical system.

A technique that some early synthesizer players adopted to create new sounds was to play the same part on two keyboards at the same time, one hand on each instrument. A keyboardist could then use each instrument to its best advantage: strings from the "string synth," brass from the "brass synth," and so on. This was an awkward technique at best, and one's polyphony was limited to the number of fingers on one hand, typically five.

Rock musicians such as Keith Emerson, shown in **Figure 1-1**, and Rick Wakeman became famous for the enormous stacks of electronic keyboards they would stand in front of and play. Joe Zawinul, of the 'seventies jazz group Weather Report, developed a unique technique for playing on two keyboards simultaneously. He placed himself between a pair of ARP 2600 synthesizers, one of which had its keyboard electronically reversed, going from high notes on the left to low notes on the right (**Figure 1-2**).

All these elaborate measures were designed to accomplish one thing—getting the most from these great new instruments. The layering of sounds upon sounds became an important tool, almost like a

trademark sound for some of these and other artists.

Then, in 1979, came the next big step: some new keyboards were coming equipped with computer interface plugs on the back. Instruments from the Oberheim, Rhodes and Roland companies could, for the first time, be connected to another of the same model of synthesizer. For example, an Oberheim OBX synthesizer could be connected to other OBXs. When you played on the keyboard of one, both would play whatever sound was programmed. This was an improvement for performers, since sounds could now be layered on top of each other while playing a single keyboard, but it didn't answer the big question of how to connect *different* instruments from *different* brands together for unique combinations.

One person who took matters into his own hands was jazz musician Herbie Hancock. Newly enthralled with the technology of synthesizers, he spent a small fortune to have many of his electronic instruments custom modified to connect with each other, allowing him to mix and match sounds any way he wished. For the first time, instruments of different makes were connected with each other by means of a common, though custom, digital connection.

More and more rock and jazz musicians were approaching the instrument makers to try and get their own equipment to interconnect. In addition, the first digital *sequencers* (a device that records and replays back a performance on an electronic musical instrument) were starting to show up. These sequencers, such as the Roland MC-4 Micro-Composer (*see* **Figure 1-3**) and the Oberheim DSX, were yet another reason to want compatibility between products from the different instrument makers. It would be possible for one person to sequence and play back all the parts of a song on a group of synthesizers. The

Figure 1-2 Joe Zawinul of the Group Weather Report

Roland Micro-Composer was a primitive, four-track sequencer that produced either control voltages, used extensively for controlling earlier analog synthesizers, or used a special "Roland only" digital connector for some of their newer instruments. Oberheim's sequencer was quite a bit more sophisticated, but was limited to use only with their own OBX model synthesizers.

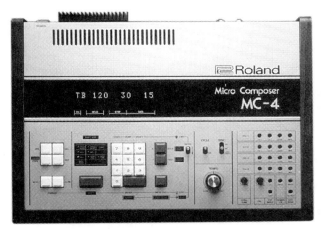

Figure 1-3 The Roland MC-4 MicroComposer

TIME FOR A CHANGE

Time was ripe for a change to occur in the musical instrument industry by the early 'eighties. Synthesizers were no longer a *techno-oddity*, and sales of instruments to the mass market musicians, as well as to professionals, were growing quickly. There were more companies involved now from Japan, the U.S. and Europe. The diversity of keyboards, drum machines, sequencers, and other musical devices was growing rapidly. To move up another notch in technology and accessibility, the synthesizer industry needed to take a lesson in compatibility from the computer industry.

Computer makers have long depended on certain technical standards to ensure compatibility between computers and other devices. For example, the *modem* is a device that lets computers exchange information over telephone lines. It makes no difference what the makes, models or cost of the interconnected computers are. Now, millions of people on thousands of different computers all speak the same "language" because their equipment was designed using the same technical standard for modems. Other examples of computer standards are disk drives, printers, cables, memory chips, and many types of software. Compatibility strengthened the new personal computer industry and was a major factor in its amazing success. There are many examples of technical standards that allow devices from different companies to work together. Look at the success of items such as VCRs, video cameras and tapes, cassette machines and tapes, stereo equipment and a host of everyday gizmos.

Twice a year, the members of the National Association of Music Merchandisers (NAMM) hold a huge convention to show new musical products and find new ways to market musical instruments and accessories. During one of these shows in 1982, a meeting of a small group of synthesizer manufacturers took place at the request of Dave Smith, President of Sequential Circuits, a popular synthesizer company of that time. Engineers from many of the major synthesizer companies were in attendance. They discussed a proposal for the adoption of a *universal standard for the transmitting and receiving of musical performance information between all types of electronic musical instruments*. The original proposal was called UMI, for *Universal Musical Interface*.

The original proposal went through a significant number of revisions before being renamed and becoming the *Musical Instrument Digital Interface*, or MIDI standard. Several prominent Japanese musical instrument companies became involved in engineering the final version. It was a truly international cooperative venture. Finally, in 1983, Sequential Circuits from the U.S. and Roland from Japan introduced the first keyboards with MIDI, soon followed by virtually every other synthesizer company in the world!

Within three years after MIDI's introduction, almost no electronic instrument was made in the world that didn't have a MIDI plug on it. It became a true universal standard. To this day there is no competition to MIDI for connecting all types of electronic musical instruments together or for creating personal musical systems. Like computers, MIDI is used by millions of people for thousands of applications. It's also being used in fields other than just music, such as theatrical lighting, computer games and recording studio automation.

From the beginning, the MIDI standard was designed with room for growth and improvement. Since its start, new features have been added, while others have been defined more clearly. A great deal of room was left for expansion without sacrificing the main power of MIDI—simplicity and compatibility with all other existing MIDI instruments.

This book is a guide for the musician, performer, producer, composer, engineer, computer enthusiast, student, or anyone wanting to get a good understanding of how MIDI works, and how to work with MIDI. It will assist you in learning the nuts and bolts of MIDI technology. The more you understand how MIDI operates, the easier it is to use the musical tools it provides. You will develop an understanding of how a MIDI system can be put together quickly and easily for any occasion.

You will gain the knowledge needed to make sound (pun intended) purchases of MIDI and MIDI-related equipment. You will learn how to get the most out of any musical situation that calls for using electronic musical instruments. Examples of many different MIDI systems are shown to help with the creation of the right music system for your needs and budget. You will probably be surprised at just how simple MIDI is to understand and use. As your knowledge about MIDI increases, you will see the wonderful possibilities available to you from the technology of music.

Synthesizer engineers see the need for MIDI.

2

The Language of Machines

Telephones and cable television use electricity to send information over wires. MIDI sends information over wires too, though in a slightly different way. MIDI uses the same technology as computers to relay information from one machine to another.

When you speak on the telephone, the microphone in your phone's handset converts the sound of your voice into electricity. The electricity travels over a single wire to the telephone on the other end of the line, which converts that electricity back into sound through the speaker in the handset. A second wire sends sound from the other phone back to yours. This is a simple circuit, *but its simplicity makes it no less powerful!*

Cable television sends even more information over a wire. Dozens of channels of information (in the form of pictures and sound) travel from the local cable company to your house over a single cable. Using the tuner on your TV or cable box, you select the one channel you want to watch. Even though all the other programs currently running are coming into your home via the cable, you are tuning them out while allowing your favorite show to appear on the TV screen. This is an example of *multi-channel* transmission.

Computers can also be connected together in order to send many kinds of data, but they do so differently (they don't have voices or game shows). One method is by using a *modem,* which connects computers via telephone lines, allowing computer users to exchange electronic mail, programs, pictures, play games, type messages, or other types of information. Unlike telephones or TV, computers communicate *digitally*, which means that they use numbers to represent everything. Computers communicate with each other via numbers. MIDI is digital too. Remember, MIDI stands for Musical Instrument *Digital* Interface.

If you already play or use synthesizers, drum machines, sequencers, digital effects, or most any electronic music equipment, you already know how to work with computers, because that's exactly what you are doing. The personal computer is but one type of computer. With synthesizers, you are simply working with a *different type of computer* in a different way—instead of producing mailing lists, you are making sounds and music.

This all leads up to a brief explanation of a few key parts of computer technology that apply directly to MIDI. *MIDI is the sending and receiving of information between two computers*, not computers that do spreadsheets, but the kind that make *music*. Let's understand what digital means a little better.

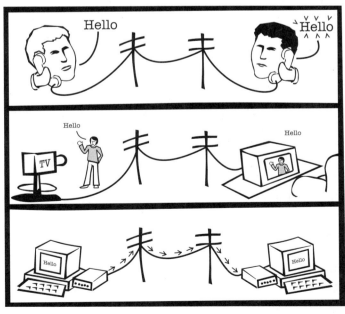

Figure 2-1

Information can be sent over wires in a number of ways.

INSIDE THE MIND OF A MACHINE

If you could see into a computer's inner workings, here's what you would find?

Computers, and all so-called "intelligent machines," are not necessarily so complex, or so smart. Computer processors (called *Central Processing Units*, or *CPUs*) are found in a wide range of everyday items from desktop personal computers (PCs), to banking machines, calculators, auto-dial telephones, video games, VCRs, and yes, MIDI synthesizers and other electronic musical instruments. All computer-based machines have the basic elements shown in **Figure 2-2**.

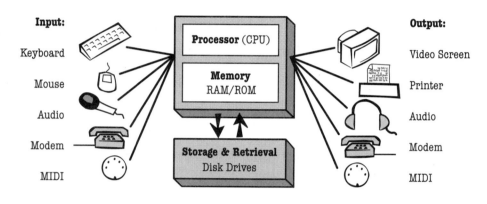

Figure 2-2
A computer system is made up of many parts.

A computer takes information from the outside world through its *input*. It then organizes it, modifies it (if called to by its *software* program), and stores it within its memory. Input can take many possible forms, depending on the nature of the machine and the desired tasks at hand. Typing on a computer keyboard, using a mouse, modem or any of the devices in **Figure 2-2** are all examples of input.

A PC displays information on its video screen with letters, words, numbers, colors or pictures, but it holds that information internally as *numbers in its memory*. That is the only way a computer stores information. In order for information to go into a computer, it must be *digitized*, i.e., turned into the numbers a computer understands. For example, as you type on a computer keyboard, the computer is converting each letter into a specific code in order to store it in its memory. In addition to text, computers can receive pictures or sounds with the proper hardware and digitize them into groups of numbers.

Once inside, these numerical codes are used by the computer to represent and store all the informa-

tion they have received. Each letter of the alphabet is a number. So is each color. More complex pictures and graphics are groups of numeric information in the computer's memory. A computer program (*software*) is a series of actions that the CPU can carry out on the information stored in the computer's memory. These actions, too, are stored as digital codes.

So, numbers are the language of machines. In order for people to understand the information inside any computer, the codes must be translated back into some language we humans understand—letters, words, pictures or sounds. That's the *output*. For example, if you wish to retrieve the information that you typed on the computer's keyboard earlier, the computer must first translate the digital codes back into the letters and numbers you typed in order to display them on its screen.

A CD player is really a specialized kind of computer. The CD disc is the input. The computer gets huge streams of numbers that are encoded on the disc and outputs them as sounds to your amplifier and speakers. A computer game is little more than pictures and a set of complex rules, all represented in the machine as numeric codes, and translated on the screen as colorful graphics and actions. In the world of computers, numbers can do just about anything.

STORING INFORMATION

How does a digital machine store a number? The answer is in small bits of electricity in the memory chips of the computer. These memory chips are called *RAM*, which stands for Random Access Memory, and they store all the information put into a computer. These bits of electricity are called, appropriately enough, *bits*. A bit is like a microscopic little switch—it is either ON or OFF. Bits are grouped and arranged inside RAM in patterns that, when added together, become numbers to the computer. Those patterns create a code that only computers can understand. It is the role of the computer to convert those patterns of electricity into information that humans can understand.

A computer doesn't look at each of the bits in its memory individually, but in uniform small groups called *bytes*. A byte represents a single numerical value to the computer, and is usually made up of 8, 16 or more bits. It's the computer's job (with the help of software) to convert those bytes into all kinds of information—including letters, numbers, symbols, graphics, sounds or commands. Musical instruments use bytes to represent program settings, front panel knob and button settings, key presses, rhythmic patterns in a drum machine and anything else the synthesizer will do or remember.

The more bits used in a byte, the bigger the range of possible numerical values it can represent. Every computer or other digital device is designed to recognize bytes of a particular bit size. More is better, but also more complex and expensive. That's one reason why there are more *and* less powerful machines available.

A computer's RAM memory is considered *volatile*, meaning it holds information only while the machine is on. If information needs to be kept after the machine is shut off, then it is necessary for another means of memory storage and retrieval to be included, such as a disk drive or memory card.

DANCING BIT TO BIT

When any two computers are connected together, either with a modem or by a more direct link, there is no need to translate the information into "human recognizable form." It can remain in digital form from output to input. A computer communicates with other computers by sending each of its stored bits electrically over a wire. A receiving computer will then store the bits in its own memory to re-form the information into numbers.

However, in order for computers to share information, a standard form of *transmission* is essential. Telephones everywhere all use the same kind of wiring, dialing system, voltages, microphones, and speakers. As a result, any phone can dial up any other phone. The same is true with computer modems. They are all compatible with each other. However, there are also other more direct ways of linking computers and other digital devices without modems or phones. It can take quite a few bits to say something important. It takes about forty bits for a computer to just to send the word "HELLO."

Some computer systems can send information over a multi-wired cable several bits, or a whole byte at a time. This technique is called *parallel transmission* and it works something like **Figure 2-3**.

Parallel transmission schemes use cables and connectors with several wires in them. Each bit of a number is sent over one of the wires in the cable. This is the most efficient way to send data between two computers.

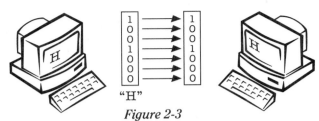

Figure 2-3
Parallel transmission sends data over several wires.

Serial transmission is another technique for sending information from computer to computer. Instead of sending several bits of information simultaneously over several wires, the bits leave the computer in a single file line over a single wire:

At the other end of the wire, the receiver picks up the bits and reassembles them into the byte of information, in this case (**Figure 2-4**) the numerical

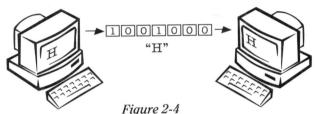

Figure 2-4
Serial transmission sends all the data over a single wire

code for the letter "H." It's called *serial* transmission since the bits are moving in a series (one after another) through the wire.

Computers, or other computer-based devices that can be linked to share information, use one of these two methods of digital communication—serial or parallel. There are advantages and drawbacks to each: While parallel transmission is more efficient and generally faster, the input and output hardware and the cables are more expensive. Longer parallel computer cables unfortunately can also act as very good radio antennae, inadvertently sending or receiving radio interference that can disrupt any nearby devices such as TVs, VCRs, radios or amplifiers. In turn, those machines can also radiate interference into a parallel cable and disrupt the data as it travels between devices. Parallel cables cannot be longer than just a few feet before the data starts to become unreliable and inaccurate.

On the other hand, serial input and output, while a bit slower due to its method of sending numbers one bit at a time, has several advantages: It is significantly less expensive to implement, the cables can be much longer, and there is no radio noise interference problem.

SENDING INFORMATION THE MIDI WAY

So what does all of this have to do with MIDI and musical instruments? The technology behind PCs and MIDI instruments is the same. Computers are composed of a microprocessor, digital memory, and some means of sending and receiving information with the outside world. Sending and receiving can either be between the computer and you, or between the computer and another computer. For example, a button pressed on the front panel of a synthesizer will cue the instrument's internal computer to do something such as change to a different sound or alter the current sound. The computer can display the new sound's name or changed parameter on the synthesizer's front panel. Recalling a stored sound (also called a *program* or *patch*) causes the synthesizer to look inside a particular part of its memory to get the various parameters of the sound, and then move them to an area to be played or changed. When a key is pressed on the keyboard of a synthesizer, the computer will interpret that to mean "play this note now!"

It is the microcomputer chip that makes modern electronic instruments sound so vivid, while so easy to use, compared with their pre-digital predecessors. Using computer technology does not automatically make things more complex, in fact it makes working with instruments much simpler. Without the memory and CPU chips that go inside instruments, it would be impossible to retrieve a stored sound at the touch of a button, as current instruments can do. It would be impossible to have a drum machine or a sequencer, or to "sample" sounds, or to have a graphic visual display on an instrument to assist in the creating of new sounds. Most kinds of sound processing such as delays and reverbs could not be produced. MIDI would not exist.

MIDI, which is a *Digital Interface* (interface is a fancy word for *connection*), must use some standard means of moving musical "data" from one instrument to another, just as computers send words and other information back and forth.

With the knowledge of parallel and serial transmission technology in mind, the creators of MIDI had an easy time deciding which kind of transmission method to use. The disadvantages of parallel outweighed its advantages, and so they chose the simpler, less expensive but more reliable, serial transmission technology.

Let's see that in big letters:

MIDI USES SERIAL TRANSMISSION

To keep things simple and inexpensive (so everyone could get their hands on it), the creators of MIDI chose a simple, readily-available five pin plug to put on all MIDI-compatible instruments and cables, called a *DIN plug*. It had been used previously for many applications in audio and video, but none involving electronic musical instruments. Thus, it would not be confused with other connectors found in music studios, such as audio or electrical cables, but people could buy them at their nearby electronics store. The MIDI connectors found on every MIDI instrument and cable look like this:

Figure 2-5
A standard MIDI Connector with 5 pins

The plugs on the instruments are "female" with five small holes, while the cables are "male" with 5 matching pins on both ends. On all MIDI plugs and cables, opposite the five little connectors, is a small notch that helps you align the small pins on the cable with the corresponding holes on the plug. MIDI cables can be found in many lengths, from 1 foot up to about 50 feet (15 meters), which handle most needs.

Since serial data transmission needs only a single wire to send information from machine to machine, why are there five wires in a MIDI cable?

Not all the pins and wires are used:

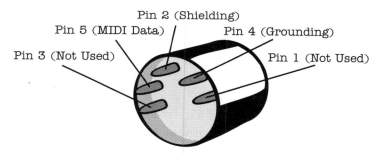

Figure 2-6
Not all pins are used on a MIDI cable

- Pin 1 and Pin 3 are not used at all. In most MIDI cables, they are not even connected to the wires.

- Pin 2 is used as electrical shielding. That means it is attached to a wire that is wrapped around all the other wires in the cable. This important feature helps prevent the cable from transmitting or receiving any kind of electrical or radio interference that might ruin the data as it travels down the cable.

- Pin 4 is a grounding wire. Grounding is a part of most electric circuits to ensure that the electricity flows in the proper direction.

- Pin 5 is the only real sender of MIDI information!!

Since MIDI uses a single wire in the cable to send information, the musical data that MIDI sends travels in only one direction over a single cable. However, MIDI was devised to allow information to go both directions between two instruments, by simply using two cables. At the same time, MIDI can also pass data on to a third, fourth, fifth instrument, or as many synthesizers as you can afford. To accomplish this, it was decided to have three different MIDI connectors on each instrument:

- One to receive data IN,

- One to send the data OUT,

- One to pass incoming data on THROUGH (spelled "THRU" in the MIDI world) to another MIDI instrument.

Here is what a typical MIDI instrument's MIDI connectors (also called "ports") look like:

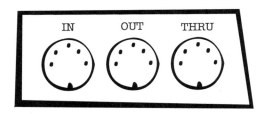

Figure 2-7
Most MIDI devices have these three connectors

Three plugs—IN, OUT, and THRU—are located on the backs of virtually every MIDI instrument or device. To prevent the possible electrical problems that can cause hum in an audio system, all MIDI ports are *opto-isolated*, which means they convert electricity to light and back to electricity at each port. This keeps each instrument electrically isolated from the others. Understanding what each connector does lets you see the logic behind putting a MIDI system together.

MIDI OUT

Perhaps the most important concept to understand is that ***MIDI does not transmit sound*** over wires the way audio components in a stereo system do. Instead, it sends digital codes that *represent what is being played on the instrument*. As you play on a MIDI keyboard, your *performance* is examined by the computer in the instrument. Your actions are then translated by the instrument's computer into a stream of MIDI codes. That information is sent out the instrument's MIDI OUT port to other synthesizers that reproduce the performance, but using sounds of their own.

MIDI IN

MIDI keyboards can be viewed as being two machines in one: One is the computer processor that monitors the keyboard, program memory, front panel displays and MIDI ports. The other part, under the control of the on-board computer, is the electronics that actually make the sounds.

The MIDI IN port receives incoming MIDI information and sends it to the instrument's computer. Once there, it is analyzed and acted upon the same as a performance *on* the instrument itself, such as pressing a key to play a note. There is little or no difference to the sound-making part of a synthesizer, whether the command to play a note comes from a key press on the instrument itself, or comes as a command via the MIDI IN port.

MIDI THRU

In order to send MIDI data on to other instruments in a chain, a third MIDI connector called THRU duplicates any MIDI messages that come to the MIDI IN port of an instrument. It is a "repeater" of the MIDI data. An important concept to understand when putting together a MIDI-based music system is that *anything played on a keyboard only goes out the MIDI OUT, and not the MIDI THRU.*

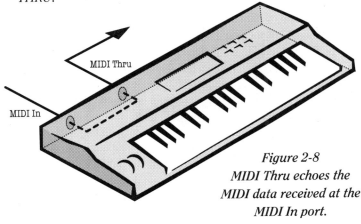

Figure 2-8
MIDI Thru echoes the MIDI data received at the MIDI In port.

Like the symbols in hieroglyphics, the dots and dashes of Morse code, or the tones in a Touch Tone phone, the bytes in a computer are a *code*. MIDI information is a computer code as well. Every time a key is pressed or a pitch wheel is moved, one or more bytes are sent out an instrument's MIDI OUT port. Other synthesizers connected to that sending instrument are looking for those bytes to come over the wire, which are then interpreted back into commands for the synthesizer to obey. Digital codes are *messages* to a computer, just like the words in a phone call or the letters on this page are to a person. Some messages are interpreted as commands ("do something now!") and others as information ("the last note played was a C♯")

When computers are connected to share these codes they form a *network*. MIDI is a network for musical instruments.

FAST AND FASTER

MIDI sends information at a rate of 31,250 bits per second. This speed is called a *baud rate*. Sometimes it is referred to as 31.25 Kbaud, which stands for *kilobaud*, meaning thousands of bits per second. Since MIDI is serial, it sends data one bit at a time. All MIDI messages use 8 bits for the information. To guarantee perfect accuracy when MIDI data is being transmitted, two additional bits are used in every byte, bringing the total up to ten bits per MIDI message byte. Which means that MIDI sends about three bytes of data every *millisecond* (one thousandth of a second).

MIDI data moves in a single direction through the cable (as seen through a high power microscope).

The MIDI message for playing a single note has three bytes in it. At the MIDI speed of 31,250 bits per second, it will take .96 milliseconds to send the command to play a note from one instrument to another. To keep things simple, this number is rounded off and called one millisecond. It takes another three bytes–another millisecond–to shut that note off. If it takes one millisecond to turn the note on and one to turn the note off, then MIDI can play approximately 500 notes a second—a lot of notes!

However, the ear is highly sensitive. It can detect if two sounds are played simultaneously or if they are slightly apart in time. How slightly? Many people feel that when there's a gap of less than 20 to 30 milliseconds between two sounds, they are perceived as sounding simultaneously. As the time gap gets longer, the ear will perceive it as two sounds. This is still well outside the time delay factors in MIDI. The data for an eight-note chord will take only about four milliseconds to transmit over MIDI. Even large chords, though transmitted serially, still sound simultaneous. With these numbers, assume that even very complex music sent over MIDI should be heard exactly as it was played.

Some of this depends on the types of sounds being used. Complex music using sounds with fast, clicky attacks might begin to have some noticeable timing delays. If the same music were to use sounds with slower attacks, such as slow string or brass sounds, no delays would be perceived.

From the start, there has been a bit of controversy over MIDI's speed and accuracy. Is it fast enough? Should it be replaced with something faster? For most music systems, it works perfectly. The occasional tiny time lags that may occur in some people's MIDI systems are more often due to the instruments themselves, rather than MIDI's speed and efficiency. The speed of a MIDI instrument's built-in microprocessor to respond to MIDI information, process it and begin the actual note is greater in some instruments than others. Some cars have more horsepower and some synthesizers respond to MIDI faster. Most instruments are amazingly fast at responding to MIDI, and the vast majority of people using MIDI have no problems at all with the speed or timing accuracy of their music systems.

Those three connectors—IN, OUT, and THRU—are the backbone of all MIDI hardware. Understanding these will give you the basis for being able to put together a MIDI system to suit any purpose. Now, look at what is actually communicated between instruments over MIDI.

What MIDI Sends – A Musical Breakdown

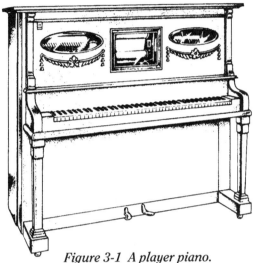

Figure 3-1 A player piano.

The old player piano—a marvel of technology in its time: A roll of paper with holes in it passes over a metal bar. There are holes in the metal bar, one for each of the 88 keys on the piano. A vacuum pump inside the piano draws air in through the holes in the bar. When a hole in the paper comes over a hole in the bar, air is allowed in, which then triggers a mechanism to move the hammer onto the appropriate string and strike the note. There was a special recording piano built solely for creating the paper rolls. The player pianos that people bought for their homes were for playback only, not unlike a record or CD player. As far as dynamics or musical nuance were concerned, they didn't exist on the player piano. Each key was struck with exactly the same force, creating a performance that might at best be called forceful, and at worst cacophonous. They were still a hi-tech wonder of their day.

What was "encoded" on the player piano's paper rolls wasn't the actual sound of a piano, but simply what was *played* on the piano. The main idea behind MIDI is the same: to allow what is *performed* on one MIDI instrument to be played on any other MIDI instrument. Your physical actions are analyzed by the instrument's computer and converted into a series of codes that are then sent out of your instrument's MIDI OUT port over a MIDI cable to all other MIDI instruments that are connected to yours. They will play exactly what you are playing, but with their own sounds. In essence, the instrument you are playing, which is called the *master*, controls all the other instruments in the system, which are the *slaves*. It's as if another player was sitting at each instrument and playing it exactly in time with you. MIDI allows for nearly unlimited connection and layering of electronic instrumental sounds.

MIDI doesn't just stop at layering different synthesizers together. It is also used for recording your musical performances for playback later, like a tape recorder, but far more powerful and fun. Instead of recording sounds to a tape, which allows for very little in the way of further editing, MIDI data can be recorded into special MIDI recording devices or computers. This is called *sequencing*. Once recorded into a sequencer, your performance can be edited in any number of ways and replayed back by any other MIDI

15

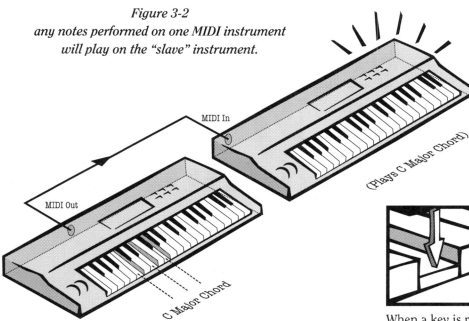

Figure 3-2
any notes performed on one MIDI instrument will play on the "slave" instrument.

MIDI In

MIDI Out

(Plays C Major Chord)

C Major Chord

instrument or connected instruments. If you wish, MIDI lets you be your own band or orchestra. You are limited only by your imagination and budget.

The word MIDI has really come to mean two things: The first is hardware—the plugs and cables found on all MIDI instruments used for the transmitting of musical data. But MIDI also refers to the digital codes themselves sent out over the MIDI cables from instrument to instrument.

Each piece of equipment in a MIDI setup plays a specific role in the system. There are transmitters, which send MIDI data, and there are receivers, which get and respond to MIDI data, as shown in **Figure 3-2**. Some instruments do both, while some do just one or the other.

MIDI's original design was based around the keyboard as a means of performance control, but its usefulness goes far beyond that one type of instrument. There are MIDI controllers for guitarists, drummers, woodwind players, and violinists. These devices are played like their traditional models, but their job is to generate MIDI information. MIDI has allowed for the creation of new kinds of instruments that never existed before. MIDI is also used for some non-musical applications as well, such as operating and automating theatrical lighting gear, or automating recording studio and video post-production equipment.

You've seen the hardware side of MIDI. Now here's a look at the software side—the codes that come from a musical performance. These are the main elements of the MIDI code...

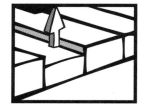

PRESSING A KEY

When a key is pressed on a MIDI controller, such as a keyboard, a digital message is sent out that says:

"A key has just been pressed!"

That simple message will command a slave synthesizer to play a note. The message is followed by two more pieces of information: The first says *which* key was pressed (middle C, or A flat below middle C, etc.). The second one indicates *how quickly* that key was pressed (velocity), which tells other instruments the dynamic (loudness or softness) of the note just played.

RELEASING A KEY

MIDI treats the pressing of a key and the releasing of a key as two different events. MIDI instruments don't know the length of time that a key is held down. Every MIDI message is sent out just as the action occurs. The moment a key is pressed, the code indicating that action is sent. The moment a key is released, *another* code is sent to indicate that movement.

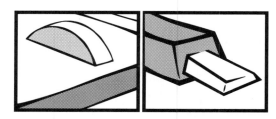

WHEELS AND PEDALS

Typical MIDI instruments have one or more knobs, wheels, pedals, or levers to control various musically expressive synthesizer parameters such as *pitch bending*, *modulation*, and *sustain*. In MIDI these are called *Continuous Controllers*, and each of these has its own special code:

There is a MIDI code for the *pitch bend wheel*, which is a wheel or lever found on most synthesizers for bending a note slightly. Whenever it is moved up or down, a code is sent out. The code does not say what the note is, nor how far the pitch is bent, it simply represents the current position of the pitch bend wheel.

Most keyboards have a *modulation wheel* or *lever* for adding vibrato to a sound. MIDI has a code for the movement of the wheel; the farther the wheel is turned, the larger the value of the code, and the more intense the vibrato.

KEY PRESSURE

Many MIDI keyboards can sense if pressure is applied to a key after it has been struck. This is called *aftertouch,* and is used for effects such as vibrato or brightness. MIDI has two different codes for aftertouch: One sends a value for the entire keyboard. The second one can send an individual value for each key. Because of the expense of putting an aftertouch sensor under each key, this second code is rarely used.

PROGRAMS

Nearly all MIDI devices have some sort of memory. Synthesizers remember sounds, drum machines remember rhythmic patterns, and effects processors remember parameter settings. These sets of stored information are called *programs* or *patches*. There is a code in MIDI called *Program Change* that tells an instrument to change to a specific program number in its memory.

PEDALS AND SWITCHES

Like pianos, most synthesizers use pedals for sustaining notes played on the keyboard and for other functions. Some of the *Continuous Controllers (see page39)* in MIDI are used specifically for pedals and switches. Like the keys on a keyboard, a code is sent when the pedal is pressed, and another is sent when it is released. Other Continuous Controllers messages are used for setting overall volume, balance, breath control, panning controls, and controlling the depth of external audio effects. They can be sent by additional sliders on a synthesizer, or by other special MIDI devices.

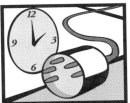

SYNCHRONIZING

Sequencers and drum machines are special MIDI devices for music recording and playback. They have built-in timing clocks that let you set them to a desired tempo. They can be synchronized automatically by MIDI messages called *System Real Time*. Real time messages are sent out in time with the music—the faster the song, the faster the messages are sent. They allow one device to tell another when to start, when to stop, how fast to play, when to change tempo, where to begin within a piece, and other information.

SPECIAL INFORMATION

The memory inside of MIDI instruments stores information about the patches as a list of *parameters*. The parameters are unique for each instrument, but include information about waveforms, brightness of the sound, and many other timbral elements of the patch. A set of MIDI messages called *System Exclusive* allows this special information to be sent between similar instruments (ones that can use the same programs) and also from instruments into computers. Here, the synthesizer patches can be stored and edited with the proper software. For example, samplers (instruments that record acoustic sounds into digital memory and then play them back) can use a special System Exclusive code called *Sample Dump Standard* to send sounds to other samplers or to computers.

MIDI performs other non-musical tasks that have special System Exclusive codes. These messages can operate video and audio recording equipment, or automate theatrical lighting and other functions that require precise timing.

MISCELLANEOUS

There are a few other MIDI commands for handling special situations. For example, *MIDI Time Code* is a special MIDI message used to synchronize MIDI devices with video or audio tape, and is used in film and TV production. There are a few special *Mode Messages* which are used in MIDI to control the way an instrument responds to MIDI.

RECOMMENDED PRACTICES

Finally, there are parts of MIDI that send no messages at all. They are called *recommended practices*, and their role is to enhance compatibility among various MIDI instruments and other devices. They are not required by any instrument, but are simply suggestions made to all MIDI instrument manufacturers to help their products work better in any MIDI system.

SUMMARY

MIDI breaks a musician's performance into many very small parts and converts it into a series of special messages. Those messages are transmitted from a master controller to any number of other instruments in a way that makes it possible to reproduce exactly the original performance. Not all MIDI instruments have all the features listed above, and there are still a few more elements yet to be discussed. Each instrument or device has a specific function in a MIDI system. As you will see in the next chapters, MIDI is a powerful, easy to use, and well-designed system that does not sacrifice simplicity for its abilities.

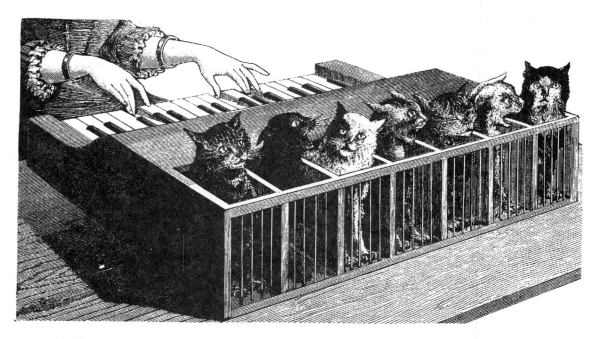

MIDI instruments use many techniques for sound production. Please don't try this at home.

4

The MIDI Studio

As you will see, MIDI lets you put together a personalized music system to do whatever you please. Your musical interests may be in pop, rock, classical, rap, or dance music. You may be a songwriter, film or television composer, lounge singer, musical hobbyist, or someone just interested in playing the blues on the weekends. In any case, the technology of MIDI and electronic instruments lets you "do your thing" almost any way you want. One of the best aspects of the personal MIDI studio is that it is *personal*. You get to design it in any configuration—a piece at a time. If you like loud music, you can buy the amplifier and speakers that will handle high power. If you sing, you can get the tape machine and microphone that suits you best.

Here's a look at the components in a MIDI studio. Each piece of equipment plays a specific role in getting your musical ideas onto tape.

SYNTHESIZERS

The synthesizer can be considered in some ways the "ultimate musical instrument." Most contemporary synthesizers not only can create a wide palette of unique and interesting sounds, but can emulate everything from grand pianos and church organs to entire symphony orchestras.

Today's synthesizers come in many shapes, sizes and audio colors. Because there are many technolo-

gies available for creating sound, different synthesizers have unique sonic personalities. Some are more sonically versatile than others. They also come in a wide price range. Some synthesizers have piano-style keyboards with up to 88 keys. Other synthesizers, called *synthesizer modules*, are simply boxes that can be mounted onto a standard 19" width rack. They are controlled entirely by MIDI, and have front panel controls and displays for programming sounds. Some synthesizers are highly programmable, offering you numerous parameters for creating and modifying your own library of sounds, while others are more limited in their programmability, and provide only a modest set of parameters for making changes to their preset sounds.

Synthesizers all have some limit to the number of notes they can play at one time, called their *polyphony*. Some synthesizers are capable of producing only one tone color (called a *timbre*) at a time, while others are able to reproduce several timbres at once. These instruments are called *multitimbral* synthesizers. With the proper MIDI system, a single multitimbral synthesizer can play up to 16 parts simultaneously, such as piano, bass, strings and drums. Such versatility in a single instrument is very useful.

Most synthesizers come with dozens or even hundreds of preset programs. You can also program your own custom sounds. Programs are stored on small memory cards, which are not interchangeable between instruments. If you are not interested in creating your own sounds, there are many companies who sell sounds for most popular synthesizers. Some synthesizers come with built-in sequencers (see *Sequencers* and *Workstations* on following page) and digital effects, making them very powerful and versatile.

SAMPLERS

Unlike a synthesizer, which creates sound electronically with special circuits called *oscillators*, a sampler creates music by digitally recording real sounds and then playing them back. A sampler has RAM memory to store recorded waveforms, which then can be saved onto computer disks. By pressing keys, those waveforms are played back at any pitch desired. Samplers can reproduce any sound that can be recorded, from the human voice, to drums, to an entire symphony orchestra, to trash cans being smashed together. The entire world becomes music with the use of samplers, which are used widely in all styles of music. The recorded sounds can be programmed and mutated to play back in many different ways, to the point that the original source is no longer recognizable and a new sound has been invented. If you are not interested in combing the world for the perfect sound, many companies sell disks with pre-recorded and programmed samples.

Like synthesizers, samplers have limited polyphony. They also have a limit to the amount of sounds they can hold at one time. Many samplers come with a small amount of memory, but can be expanded with additional memory chips.

Many synthesizers are little more than samplers that play back pre-recorded sampled sounds, but don't record.

SEQUENCERS

MIDI sequencers are the heart of most MIDI-based studios. Unless you plan to only play live in front of an audience or tape, you will want a sequencer of some kind. Sequencers work like a cross between a multitrack tape recorder and a computer. Instead of recording sounds like a tape recorder does, they record and playback MIDI data. Sequencers are more powerful than tape recorders in that they allow you to edit out mistakes, play music in slowly, change keys without replaying parts, and rearrange an entire

song with just a few button presses.

Sequencers can either be software or hardware based. Software-based sequencers are programs that require a personal computer to operate. MIDI sequencers are available for all popular computers. Hardware, or "stand-alone" sequencers are complete by themselves. They are more compact and portable than computer sequencers, but are not as versatile for editing the music inside the machine. Some hardware sequencers come with synthesizer and drum machine capabilities built in, making them ideal for live music situations where a prerecorded accompaniment is needed.

Computer-based sequencers have the advantage of a large screen and usually have more features. Most software sequencers can exchange their sequence files and many provide transcription into standard printed music notation.

DRUM MACHINES

First a joke...

Q: *"How many drummers does it take to screw in a light bulb?"*

A: *"None, they have machines to do that now!" (rimshot!)*

But seriously folks, the drum machine is a combination of a sampler filled with drum and percussion sounds, and a sequencer that has been optimized for creating rhythm patterns. Unlike keyboards and sequencers, drum machines have small pads on them that you can hit with sticks or your fingers to perform and record rhythm patterns. Patterns are short rhythmic phrases of usually just a few bars. The drum machine's on-board sequencer repeats the phrase over and over, and lets you record or erase parts one or two instruments at a time. After you create a pattern for each part of the song (intro, verse, chorus, etc.), or use the ones built into the drum machine, you chain the patterns together to build the final song (well, the drum part to the song anyway).

Also available to MIDI percussionists are MIDI drum modules—basically playback-only samplers that are filled with drum and percussion sounds to be triggered via MIDI from another sequencer. Some are expandable with banks of new sounds on memory cards, while others are not.

controllers come in widths up to 88 keys, like a concert grand piano.

There are a number of other non-keyboard controllers, including MIDI drum kits, MIDI guitar controllers and MIDI wind instruments.

MIXERS

WORKSTATIONS

For those musicians who don't want to invest in an entire room full of MIDI equipment, who want something portable enough to take traveling, or only want one basic machine with which to write songs, there is the *MIDI workstation*. It combines a little bit of everything you need to compose and play music in a single package. Workstations are multitimbral keyboard synthesizers, with sequencing, drum machines and digital effects all rolled into one instrument.

While this may sound like a perfect instrument, there are some tradeoffs in exchange for this power and portability. The sequencers in all but the most expensive workstations are limited in the amount of music they can record, and the ability to edit musical mistakes is also more limited. Because all the sound coming from a workstation is merged together into stereo, music can be a bit more difficult to record to some tape machines. The onboard digital effects in MIDI workstations are also more limited than those available from a collection of several MIDI instruments. Still, the MIDI workstation is a practical and cost–effective tool.

Once you have several instruments in your system, you need a way to blend their audio outputs together in order to record them to a stereo tape. This requires an *audio mixer*. A mixer has four or more audio inputs, and two audio outputs. The number of inputs you will need depends on the number of instruments you plan to have in your system. Finding a mixer that fits your needs can be one of the most important purchases for a home studio. Good ones are expensive, but there is a wide range of mixers with something available in almost any price range. It's best to get something with some extra inputs, so you will have room to grow.

Most mixers also provide *EQ*, which lets you add or subtract bass and treble from an individual sound. Another function of an audio mixer is to blend individual sounds with some kinds of *effects*, such as reverb, delay or chorus, using a feature called an *effects send* or *auxiliary send*. Mixers can have two or more effects sends. Those who plan to use multitrack tape recorders will also want a mixer with an adequate number of *busses*, which send the sound from your instruments to specific tracks of the tape.

MASTER CONTROLLERS

Not all MIDI keyboards have synthesizers in them. Some do nothing but send out MIDI data to waiting synthesizer modules. These *master controllers* are often more sophisticated in their MIDI capabilities, and are popular with musicians with racks of MIDI synthesizer and sampler modules. Master keyboard

SPEAKERS

In order to hear your music, you'll want a pair of good quality speakers in front of you in your studio. Speakers are available in all sizes and prices, from low-cost miniature "bookshelf" speakers to massive and expensive "theater" speakers that can accurately simulate the sound of a jet taking off at 10 yards, and inflict about the same amount of damage to your ears. You'll probably want something inbetween those, and there are plenty to choose from.

Headphones are another way to listen to your music, but can become tiring after a while. They are usually not an accurate reflection of how your music will sound on a conventional sound system. However, your neighbors will probably buy you some if you choose the bigger speakers previously mentioned.

AMPLIFIERS

To use speakers in your studio, you will need to have some kind of amplifier. The output of your mixing console goes to the amplifier, which, in turn, is connected to the speakers. You can use a standard stereo system as an amplifier, or go for a dedicated amplifier. Amplifiers come in different power configurations, rated in *watts*. More is better, not just for loudness, but for sonic accuracy and lack of distortion as well.

DIGITAL EFFECTS

Though many synthesizers and workstations have built-in *digital effects*, often they are not enough to handle all your needs. Digital effects add ambience and spaciousness to your instrument's sound. They are also used to add a bit of spice to some sounds by adding thickness, movement, distance or other modifications. Digital effects are vital for good-sounding vocals, acoustic instruments and drums. Some effects devices provide a single effect, such as chorus, reverb or delay, while others are *multi-effects* devices, which can do many different effects at one time. Usually, you need a separate effects unit for every part you wish to process. Some digital effects can respond to MIDI messages, allowing them to change their parameters dynamically.

TAPE RECORDERS

While synthesizers and samplers are wonderful musical tools, they don't necessarily replace the use of acoustic instruments such as guitar, sax, trumpet or other more unusual instruments. If you write songs, you'll need to record vocals as well. For all of this you'll need a multitrack tape recorder. These are available in 4, 8, 12, 16, 24, 32, 48, and 64 tracks. Some small multitracks come with their own built-in mixers, but most will require an additional mixer. Multitrack recorders are available using either analog or digital recording technology.

After you've recorded your music, you'll need a stereo tape machine to record the final mix. This can be as simple as a cassette machine, or more elaborate with DAT (Digital Audio Tape) or MD (Mini Disc). Those involved in film or video scoring may want to acquire some 4-track reel-to-reel recorders or *time code DAT machines*. A more expensive option is a CD recorder, which lets you record directly onto a special CD disc that can be played on any CD player. A very impressive way to submit a demo!

DIGITAL AUDIO WORKSTATIONS

While not a replacement (yet) for multitrack recorders, Digital Audio Workstations (DAWs), which record sound directly onto computer hard disks, are a powerful addition to both home and professional studios. Available in most any configuration of tracks, DAWs not only record music, but perform complex edits on it as well, something difficult or impossible on audio tape recorders.

Some DAWs are a separate hardware device, while some are peripherals for your own computer. A DAW can record any audio, slice it up into smaller sections and rearrange the parts in any order. Sections of a track or an entire mix can be repeated without rerecording, and edits are seamless and inaudible. Some DAW systems can be operated from within a MIDI sequencer, which allows you to record both MIDI and digital audio in one file, and still be able to perform edits on all the parts together. This is a very powerful system for musicians wishing to add acoustic parts or vocals to a MIDI sequence, and also wanting the ability to go back and edit the music.

MICROPHONES

Microphones are necessary to record vocals or acoustic instruments to tape. As with almost everything in life, they are available in a wide price range and you usually get what you pay for. Many home studios get by with just one microphone for all applications, while some people may find certain mics work better for particular instruments.

THE ROOM

A home studio needs a good space. It should be quiet and comfortable. It needs enough room, not only for the equipment you have, but also some room to grow. And of course, it needs room for you.

Careful thought should be given to your equipment layout. You should have most everything you need within arm's reach, so you don't need to run around just to make music (unless you need the exercise).

EXTRAS

There are always a few extra items to put on your shopping list for your studio. Some are more important than others, but some are essential to get the job done:

MIDI cables	AC power strips
audio cables	audio patch bays
memory cards	MIDI patch bay
MIDI *thru* box	VCR
instrument stands	foot pedals
instrument racks	noise gates
travel cases	tape synchronizer
microphones	other software

An example of early amplifier design (now illegal in most states).

5

The Basics

Yiou've taken a brief look inside the wonderful world of microprocessors, memory and computer codes—the numbers used by machines to represent information. These are also the building blocks of MIDI. MIDI uses numbers to represent musical actions, such as pressing keys or pedals on a synthesizer keyboard. But MIDI does far, far more. In this chapter, you'll see how the message codes are organized in MIDI. These messages are the commands sent and received by MIDI instruments. To keep things simple, you'll learn the structure of MIDI without using the numbers themselves, leaving the actual numbers to the computers, since rarely is it necessary to know them. If you want to see the actual numbers sent by MIDI, they all appear in the *Appendix*.

As mentioned in *Chapter 2*, all MIDI instruments and devices use simple, eight-bit microprocessors to send and process MIDI data. In an eight-bit world, a computer device can process numbers from 0 to 255. In order for MIDI to get the most mileage out of an eight-bit number system, MIDI messages come in two different flavors, called *status* and *data*.

Status messages describe the *kind* of information being sent. They tell the other instruments whether the event that just occurred was a key press, a pitch wheel, or another type of performance action. When the action occurs, this is always the first code number sent by a MIDI instrument. The status message contains something called *channel* information within it, which you'll see later in this chapter.

Data messages follow status messages with the actual *values* for the event. For example, if a status message indicates a key has been pressed (called a *Note On message*), then the following data messages indicate *which* key was pressed, and the *velocity* with which it was struck. So a Note On message has one status message followed by two data messages. The various status messages in MIDI each have a specific number of data messages that follow them, depending on the type of information being sent.

Status and data bytes can be distinguished in MIDI by the value of the code number. The range of available numbers is split in half. Numbers from 128 to 255 are always status messages. Numbers from 0 to 127 are data. You'll notice in the following chapters that all data values for MIDI data are within the range of 0 to 127.

MIDI messages travel in small clusters, called *packets*. A packet is made up of a status message, followed by one or more data messages, when additional information is needed.

A good analogy for thinking about status and data in MIDI is a railroad train made up of an engine with a one or more cars attached:

The train's engine in **Figure 5-1** represents the *status* message sent by a MIDI instrument when a key on it is pressed.

Figure 5-1
A MIDI Message with a
Status and two Data bytes.

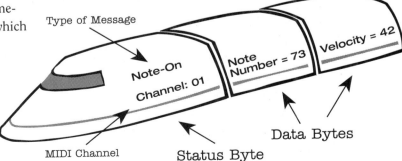

Figure 5-2
**A MIDI message with Status
and single Data bytes.**

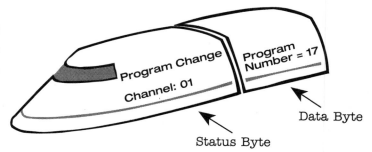

The cars of the train are the *data* messages that immediately follow the status message. They give the actual values of the event. A status message alone has no details about the event it signals, only the basic *nature* of the event (a key press, a wheel or pedal movement, etc.). The data messages provide the details, but always require a status message to tell the receiving instruments exactly *what* they are describing (see **Figure 5-2**).

When a MIDI message is received by an instrument, it is interpreted as a *command*. If an incoming message says "a note has been played" it is interpreted by the instrument as a command to "play this note NOW."

MIDI CHANNELS

MIDI has made possible the creation of personal *electronic music systems*—several different instruments working together to create your music. Sounds can be layered on top of one another with multiple instruments, and sequencers make it possible for each instrument in a single MIDI system to play a different part of a more complex composition. The ability for each instrument in a MIDI system to play a unique part is accomplished through the use of MIDI *channels*. Different musical parts, each meant to be played on different instruments, can be transmitted together over the same MIDI cable.

As a similar example, cable television can have literally hundreds of stations' signals broadcast over a single cable simultaneously. A tuner that is connected to your TV set selects a single channel at a time to watch and ignores all the rest. The TV's tuner acts as a kind of filter to let only one station's

picture and sound to pass, as shown in **Figure 5-3**.

MIDI Channels make it possible for each instrument in a system to play a unique part while connected together by a single MIDI chain. MIDI messages with different channels can be sent over a single MIDI cable simultaneously, each channel carrying a different part of the music. Each part will be played back by a synthesizer that is set to the same channel.

Instead of using frequencies like TV or radio, every MIDI message that signals an event uses a part of the *status message* to indicate the channel of the event and the data bytes that follows it:

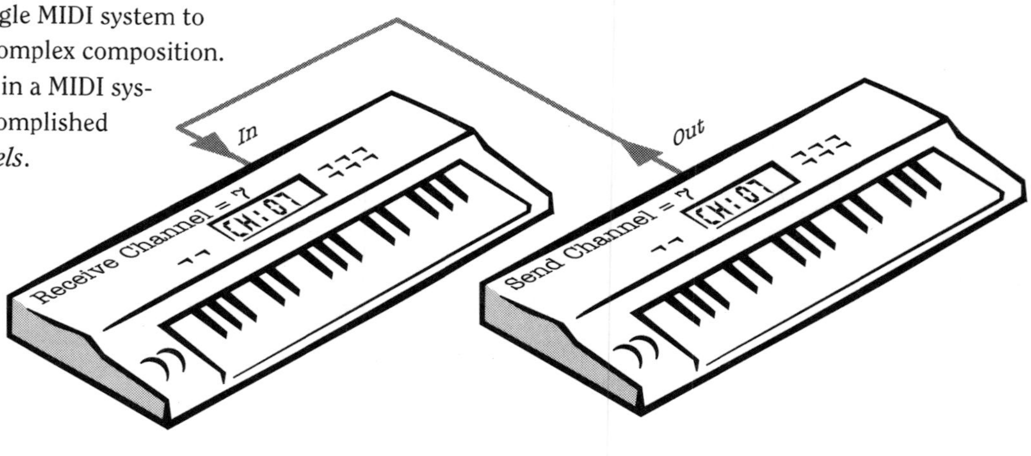

Figure 5-3
**A cable TV tuner lets you
see one channel at a time.**

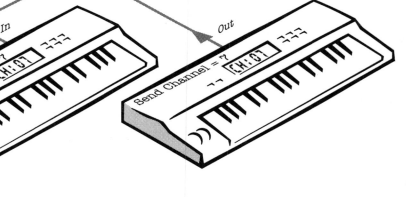

Figure 5-4
**MIDI instruments send and receive
information on Channels.**

Four of the eight bits in a MIDI status message specify the MIDI channel. Four bits have 16 possible values, and so MIDI has 16 channels available:

Bits	MIDI Channel	Bits	MIDI Channel
0000	Channel 1	1000	Channel 9
0001	Channel 2	1001	Channel 10
0010	Channel 3	1010	Channel 11
0011	Channel 4	1011	Channel 12
0100	Channel 5	1100	Channel 13
0101	Channel 6	1101	Channel 14
0110	Channel 7	1110	Channel 15
0111	Channel 8	1111	Channel 16

Figure 5-6 A synthesizer's channel selector.

All MIDI synthesizers have a way to select the channel number on which it will send and/or receive MIDI data (see **Figure 5-6**). Anything you play on a MIDI master controller is transmitted as MIDI messages on the one selected channel number. Other slave instruments in the system set to the same channel number will respond to the incoming MIDI data by playing notes, etc. Instruments set to any other channel will receive, but simply ignore the information.

Many MIDI instruments are *multitimbral*, meaning that they can play several different parts simultaneously, each with a different sound, each on a different MIDI channel. The number of available parts, up to 16, is determined by the synthesizer.

Multitimbral synthesizers select a MIDI channel and patch for each part. MIDI data coming in on a part's MIDI channel will be played by the part's current patch. Multitimbral instruments also have a *basic channel*, which is the one MIDI channel that the instrument will respond to for special global messages.

A MIDI sequencer can record and store MIDI data from all 16 channels and play them all back simultaneously over one cable connected to its MIDI OUT port. The messages on the various channels are mixed together over a single cable. A receiving MIDI instrument sees everything going over MIDI, but simply ignores incoming information on other channels.

SOUND	MIDI CHANNEL
FLUTE 1	7
ELEC PIANO	8
SLAP BASS	9

Figure 5-7 A multitimbral synth display listing several sounds and their associated MIDI channels.

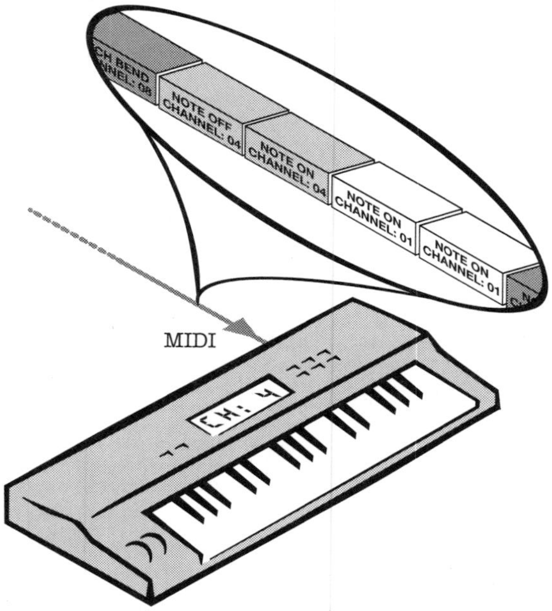

Figure 5-8
A MIDI synthesizer only responds to messages
on the same channel to which it is set.

Channels give MIDI a great deal of power and versatility. Without them, every instrument would play all the time, and sequencing multiple parts would be impossible. Since all sixteen channels can be transmitted over a single cable, you can connect many instruments to a single source without having to unplug and replug everything just to change sounds.

For the more advanced MIDI musician with a studio filled with racks of synthesizers and samplers, the limitation of 16 channels can become restrictive. Fortunately, it is possible to put together a MIDI system capable of handling more than 16 MIDI instruments or channels. Many MIDI sequencers have more than one MIDI output port, each transmitting a separate MIDI data stream with its own set of 16 channels (see *Chapter 17*).

Most MIDI keyboard controllers send data on a single MIDI channel at a time. Some instruments allow for *splits* or *zones*, in which different sections of a keyboard transmit on a different channel. This allows you to play bass with one hand and strings with another, each part played by a different instrument on a different channel. By changing the MIDI channel on your master controller, you can select one from a number of slave synthesizers that are attached. With each synthesizer in your system set to a different sound, changing the MIDI channel is like setting down your trumpet and picking up your cello (and sounding pretty good, too).

Figure 5-9
A MIDI system with synthesizers
on different channels. Only one is
used at a time.

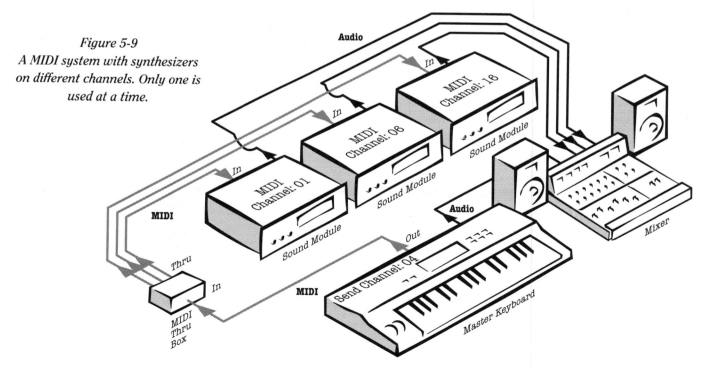

28

6

An Overview of MIDI

Now that you've taken a close look at the nature of computer codes, you can begin to see how MIDI communicates a musical performance through the language of machines. Here is a quick overview of MIDI in its entirety.

Different words are used to define MIDI—sometimes it's called a *code*, a *language*, a *protocol*, a *standard*, and a *specification*. All of these words are fine, because MIDI is technically all of these things. The word MIDI is used to describe *both* the information being sent and the way it is sent. MIDI is the messenger and the message. MIDI is a musical language (software), but also is the cables and connec-

tors (hardware) used to send the language from one device to another.

Every aspect of a musical performance is represented by its own MIDI message and accompanying data. Each message has a unique and consistent format. These formats are common to all MIDI instruments throughout the world.

Following are tables with the definition and format for all MIDI commands. The status message is shown followed by the data that accompanies it. The next chapters explain each MIDI message in greater detail.

CHANNEL VOICE MESSAGES

These are the basis of MIDI. They are for transmitting information about a musical performance:

MESSAGE	ADDITIONAL DATA*	
Note Off	key number	velocity
Note On	key number	velocity
Polyphonic Key Pressure (Polyphonic Aftertouch)	key number	pressure amount
Control Change	controller number	control value
Program Change	program number	
Channel Pressure (Channel Aftertouch)	pressure value	
Pitch Bend Change	coarse amount	fine amount

*All additional data messages have a range of 0 to 127

CHANNEL MODE MESSAGES

Channel Modes tell a synthesizer to send or receive data a certain way. The first message defines the particular mode being sent:

MESSAGE	CONTROL NUMBER	ADDITIONAL DATA
All Sound Off	120	
Reset All Controllers	121	
Local Control	122	(On /Off)
All Notes Off	123	
Omni Mode Off	124	
Omni Mode On	125	
Mono Mode On	126	number of channels (1 to 16)
Poly Mode On	127	

SYSTEM COMMON MESSAGES

These messages enhance the functions of other MIDI commands. Because they are "common," they affect all the instruments in the MIDI system, and therefore they have no channel:

MESSAGE	ADDITIONAL DATA	
MTC (MIDI Time Code)	current frame number	
Song Position Pointer	position value 1*	position value 2*
Song Select	song number (0 to 127)	
Tune Request	(none)	
End Of Exclusive Message	(none)	

* A large number is required in order to indicate that song position. For this reason, two bytes are used in the Song Position Pointer message.

SYSTEM REAL TIME MESSAGES

These commands are used for synchronizing parts of a MIDI system.
They have no channel or additional data:

MESSAGE	ADDITIONAL DATA
Timing Clock	(none)
Undefined	(none)
Start	(none)
Continue	(none)
Stop	(none)
Active Sensing	(none)
System Reset	(none)

SYSTEM EXCLUSIVE MESSAGES

These messages are used for sending and receiving an instrument's entire patch memory, sending
sample waveforms via MIDI, and several non-music event related functions:

MESSAGE	ADDITIONAL DATA	
System Exclusive	Manufacturer Identification	Followed by any amount of data
End Of Exclusive		

RECOMMENDED PRACTICES

These are not actual codes, but are add-ons to the MIDI protocol to enhance its usefulness:

Standard MIDI Files (SMF)	MIDI Machine Control
General MIDI	MIDI Show Control

These tables present a quick guide to the MIDI protocol. To see the actual code numbers used in MIDI, please refer to *Appendix 2* in the back of this book. One thing to notice from the tables is that there are three types of communication going on in MIDI:

■ *Channel Voice Messages* are only for the instruments set to a particular MIDI channel.

■ *System Common* and *Real Time* messages are for any instrument in the system.

■ *System Exclusive* data is only for a specific brand or model of device, or for special non-music oriented functions

SUMMARY

As you can see, MIDI is made up of a rather small number of command messages. Yet, together they make up the components of a complete and powerful system. MIDI has continued to grow over the years as well, adding new functions and capabilities as the demands of musicians around the world were taken into account. Seeing MIDI messages grouped by their function helps to begin seeing the logic behind MIDI.

Pre-MIDI four-voice musical instrument.

7

Channel Voice Messages

The most basic commands in MIDI are the *Channel Voice Messages*. These messages communicate the most often used performance events sent from one instrument to another over any of the sixteen MIDI channels. MIDI is capable of transmitting and reproducing every subtle nuance that even an advanced musician can perform. Yet the hardware and commands used to do this are surprisingly simple. Here are the basic MIDI messages:

NOTE ON

The primary activity in a musical performance is the playing of notes (also called *music!*). MIDI uses two separate messages, *Note On* and *Note Off*, to represent the playing of a note. 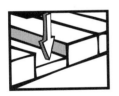 Each time you press down on a key on a MIDI keyboard (or other MIDI controller), the instrument will send out a Note On message. Any instrument connected to the sender will, at the same moment, play the same notes using its own sound-making circuitry. Note On messages are Channel Voice Messages and, therefore, sent over one of the 16 MIDI channels. Only instruments set to the same MIDI channel as the sending instrument—the one being played—will respond by making sound (see **Figure 7-1**).

There are two *data* messages that follow a Note On *status* message. The first data message is the *key number,* which is the note that was pressed. The second message is the *velocity with which the key is struck*. The harder a key is struck, the higher the velocity value that is sent over MIDI, and the louder the note. Velocity has a range of 1 to 127. Here is an example of how a Note On message is sent over MIDI:

Figure 7-2 shows a Note On on MIDI channel 1. The channel number is built into the status byte. The key number value is 64, which is "C" on the middle of the keyboard. The note played will be fairly loud with a velocity value of 102 out of possible 127.

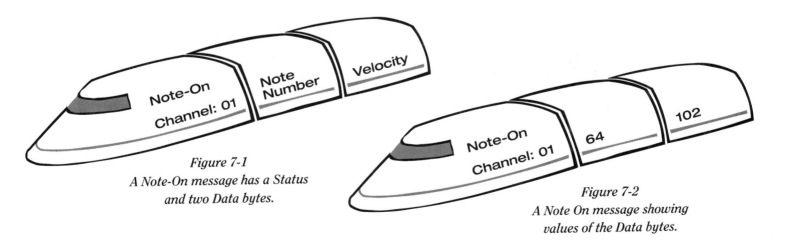

Figure 7-1
A Note-On message has a Status and two Data bytes.

Figure 7-2
A Note On message showing values of the Data bytes.

NOTE OFF

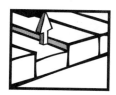

As shown in the MIDI chart on page 29, there is a separate command for Note Off, though this is rarely used in MIDI. Typically, when you release a key, another Note On command is sent with the same pitch but with a *velocity of 0*. A velocity value of 0 in MIDI always represents "a key has been released." It will cause the note playing on a receiving synthesizer to stop.

The Note Off command is only transmitted by keyboards with the capability of sensing *Release Velocity*, which is how quickly a key is released. A synthesizer uses release velocity to determine the speed of the note's *release envelope* (the synthesizer parameter that determines how quickly a note fades out after the key is released). Release velocity sensitivity is quite rare in all but the most expensive MIDI keyboards, because the extra hardware needed to detect it is costly. Note Off messages are therefore rarely seen passing through the average MIDI cable.

KEY NUMBERS

Musicians refer to notes by their letter and octave number, such as "D 3," "A♭ 6," or "C♯ 1." MIDI assigns a *Key Number* to every note of the scale with a range of 0 to 127. This is more than sufficient since a standard piano-style keyboard has no more than 88 keys. The lowest key number, "0," is "C" five octaves below middle "C." The lowest note found on a piano is two octaves higher—key number 24. After key 0

comes key number 1 (C♯), key number 2 (D), etc. Key number 127 ("G" five octaves above middle "C") is the highest value.

Though key number 60 is middle "C" on a piano keyboard, this doesn't mean that this value will always cause a middle "C" to be played by the receiving synthesizer. A synthesizer can be programmed to play any pitch, or even a drum or sound effect with no pitch at all. MIDI does not send *pitch* information, it simply sends the numbers that correspond to the keys you press on the MIDI controller. It is the synthesizer's sound settings that determine the pitch that results from a key press or MIDI Note On message.

VELOCITY

After the key number is sent in a Note On message, a data byte is sent indicating how *fast* (the velocity) the key was pressed. The receiving instrument usually translates this into the note's relative loudness. The very lowest possible value for a note's velocity is 1, which would be interpreted as *pianissimo* or "*pp*" in musical terms—very quiet. The highest value is 127, which would be *fortissimo* or "*ff*" in music—as loud as possible. Instead of being the quietest of notes possible, a velocity of 0 in a Note On message is used to represent the release of a key, or "no velocity."

A synthesizer's velocity can be used for parameters other than just loudness. It can be used to make a sound brighter, higher, lower, "bendier," or to completely change it from the way it may sound if played softly. For this reason, this data value is

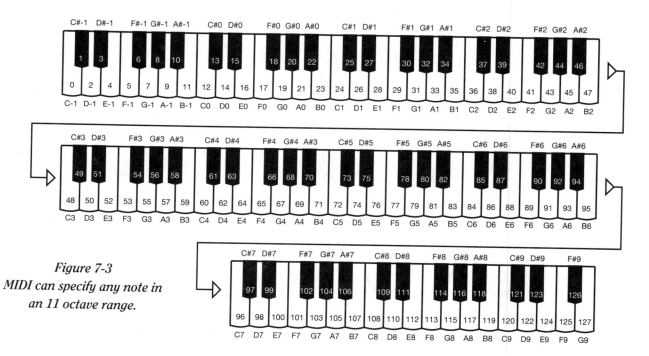

Figure 7-3
MIDI can specify any note in an 11 octave range.

always referred to as "velocity" in MIDI and never "loudness" or "volume."

Velocity is not a separate message in MIDI. It is part of the packet of data attached to every Note On status message. It cannot be omitted from Note On or Note Off messages. There are a few older MIDI keyboards that were not velocity sensitive. They use a constant, preset value for the velocity message, usually 64, right in the middle of the range.

Here is a musical example in both standard music notation and as it would be transmitted in MIDI codes from one instrument to another:

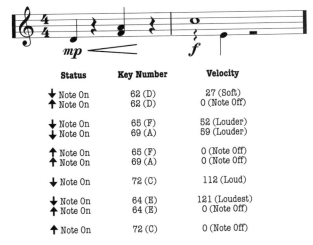

Status	Key Number	Velocity
↓ Note On	62 (D)	27 (Soft)
↑ Note On	62 (D)	0 (Note Off)
↓ Note On	65 (F)	52 (Louder)
↓ Note On	69 (A)	59 (Louder)
↑ Note On	65 (F)	0 (Note Off)
↑ Note On	69 (A)	0 (Note Off)
↓ Note On	72 (C)	112 (Loud)
↓ Note On	64 (E)	121 (Loudest)
↑ Note On	64 (E)	0 (Note Off)
↑ Note On	72 (C)	0 (Note Off)

Figure 7-4
A simple musical phrase in standard notation and in a MIDI list.

CHANNEL AFTERTOUCH

In addition to sensing the speed with which a key is pressed, many MIDI keyboards also have another sensor underneath the key bed to sense if a key is pressed even harder as it is being held down. This

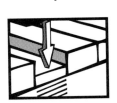

parameter is called *Aftertouch*, though "afterpress" might describe it better. Another term used is *"channel key pressure."* The Aftertouch sensor can only detect a single value for the entire keyboard. Whichever key is being pressed down the hardest will determine the Aftertouch value sent out through MIDI. As a key is pressed harder and harder, higher and higher values are transmitted in a rapid stream. If no key is being pressed, or if pressure is held steady, then no information is transmitted. Any receiving instrument set to the same MIDI channel will respond to this information, if the sound patch has been programmed to use it. Otherwise, it is ignored.

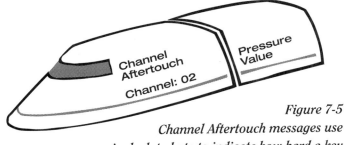

Figure 7-5
Channel Aftertouch messages use a single data byte to indicate how hard a key is being pressed.

Aftertouch is usually used for modulation (that's *vibrato* to you and me). This means that when you first play a note or chord on a synthesizer, the sound has no vibrato. Then as you press down into the keyboard, it senses the Aftertouch and commands the synthesizer to add vibrato, the depth of which is determined by how hard you press. Some synthesizers use Aftertouch for other sound parameters, such as volume or brightness. The use of Aftertouch can be very expressive and is simple to use since it does not involve taking your hands away from the keyboard.

PITCH BEND CHANGE

Those so-called "blue notes" in jazz and the blues—a slightly sharp dominant seventh and the slightly flat minor third—have for many years been exclusively in the domain of singers, guitarists, harmonica, wind, string, and brass players. Keyboardists have tried to approximate the bendy, soulful sound of blues with quick grace notes, but it isn't the same. The synthesizer's ability to bend the pitch of notes is

the stylistic liberation for keyboard players of many styles. Except for some "digital pianos" (which simulate a piano and have no added expressive controllers), few MIDI keyboards are without a pitch bend wheel or lever. Since it is an integral element of most synthesizers, it should be no surprise that part of MIDI's job is to continuously check the instrument's pitch wheel and send information about its current position to other instruments so they can duplicate it.

Figure 7-6
Pitch Bend messages use two data bytes for 16,384 possible values.

The human ear is sensitive and critical in detecting even tiny pitch variations. It can hear the difference between a tone that is gliding up or down smoothly and one that is moving in steps. Digital instruments, in fact all digital devices, think in numbers, which are like steps. In order to create the effect of a smooth transition from one pitch value to another, it is very important that the steps be as small as possible.

To ensure this, the MIDI code for pitch bend uses not one, but two bytes of information to transmit the current value. A single data message to indicate the pitch wheel's position would only have 128 possible values, and the steps between them could be audible to most people. By adding the value of the two data bytes together, MIDI gets a whopping 16,384 possible steps from the lowest position position of the wheel (the pitch bent down) to the highest (the pitch bent up).

Any MIDI instrument capable of responding to the Pitch Bend Change message, and set to the same MIDI channel as the sender, will bend all of its currently playing notes. The pitch bend *range*, also called pitch bend *sensitivity*, determines how far the pitch of notes will bend when the wheel is moved fully in one direction or the other. It is programmable on each receiving instrument, and can be different than that of the master instrument. This means that while one synthesizer may bend up or down two semitones, another one may bend seven, twelve or more semitones.

Though not used often, there is a special MIDI message that sets the pitch bend sensitivity in a slave instrument. Thus, it's your responsibility to see that the pitch bend range of all the instruments in your MIDI system are matched.

PROGRAM CHANGE

The sounds programmed into the memories of electronic instruments are variously called *programs, patches, tones,* and sometimes *performances*. Instrument manufacturers seem to delight in coming up with new names that mean the same thing—a

sound stored in a synthesizer. Instruments can have a few dozen to several hundred patch memories, though most have 128 or fewer. Any sound can be recalled by the press of a button on the front of the instrument, and is ready to play. When you press a patch button, two things happen: First, the instrument gets the sound from its memory and prepares it to play.

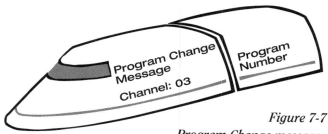

Figure 7-7
Program Change messages allow recall of up to 128 different sounds on any MIDI channel.

Second, it sends the *number of the patch* you selected out through MIDI. Other instruments in the system set to the same MIDI channel as the sender will recall the same number patch. Remember, just the *number* of the program is sent, not the parameters of the sound itself.

Different synthesizers have different schemes for organizing and numbering patches. Some use banks of 99 sounds, some have eight banks of eight sounds each, some have one or two banks of 32 or 64 sounds, and some begin numbering with 1 while others use 0. Regardless of any individual instrument's numbering method, MIDI Program change is consistent—patches are numbered 0 to 127 in MIDI. Whatever the first patch number is on the instrument sending MIDI, the data will be 0, the second patch will send 1, and so on. The same is true of receiving instruments. When a Program Change message is received with a data byte of 0, the first memory number will be recalled and ready to be played.

When working with a MIDI sequencer, you can have a single synthesizer fill multiple roles in a song by changing patches at different times during the music. The synthesizer can play strings for a few bars, and then with a single Program Change message become a choral line. By recording Program Changes into your sequencer, you are, in essence, automating the recall of sounds in your music. In a live performance situation, a single button press can call up new sounds on all the instruments in the system.

There is no standard scheme to the way sounds are organized in the synthesizers you buy. Patch 1 in one instrument may be grand piano, while in another it might be whispering voices (the exception to this can be found in the chapter on *General MIDI*). You can rearrange the patches to suit your needs if desired, but many instruments also provide *patch maps*, which allow you to choose which patch is recalled for each MIDI Patch Change value.

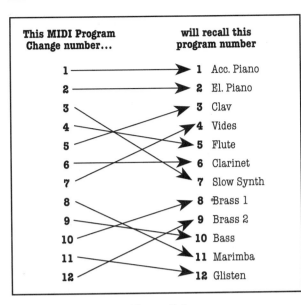

This MIDI Program Change number...	will recall this program number
1 →	1 Acc. Piano
2 →	2 El. Piano
3	3 Clav
4	4 Vides
5	5 Flute
6	6 Clarinet
7	7 Slow Synth
8	8 Brass 1
9	9 Brass 2
10	10 Bass
11	11 Marimba
12	12 Glisten

Figure 7-8
A Synthesizer Patch Map.

POLYPHONIC KEY PRESSURE

As previously mentioned, Channel Key Pressure, or Aftertouch, consists of the status message followed by one byte of value data indicating the amount of pressure being applied to the MIDI keyboard.

With *Polyphonic Key Pressure*, also called *Polyphonic Aftertouch,* each key has its own *individual* pressure level. This gives an instrument far more expressivity, but also adds far more cost, since each key must have an individual Aftertouch sensor under it. So Polyphonic Aftertouch is found only in the most expensive MIDI keyboard controllers.

There is an individual MIDI message specifically to describe this kind of Aftertouch separately from Channel Aftertouch. The status message for Polyphonic Key Pressure, which includes the MIDI channel of the message, is sent along with the key number, just like a Note On or Note Off message. It also includes a second data message, which is the current pressure value for that individual key.

For example, you could play a chord and have an individual note within it become brighter, increase its vibrato or get louder by pressing down only on that key. Or you could hold a chord while a melody note above it had vibrato added from Aftertouch. With the more common Channel Aftertouch, pressing on the one melody note key would add vibrato to all the notes playing. Synthesizers not capable of responding to the Polyphonic Aftertouch message will ignore it.

RUNNING STATUS

In **Figure 7-4** you can see how every musical event is transmitted by MIDI with a packet of a few bytes, comprised of a Status Message and one or two data messages. If only one type of message is being transmitted, such as the notes being played only on Channel 1 in the example, then every status message is the same. It is redundant when this happens, and shows that MIDI is perhaps not always as efficient as it could be at transmitting just a few simple note events.

What if it were possible to play notes and send other kinds of MIDI information in fewer messages? The overall efficiency of MIDI would improve, because more messages could be sent in less time. Eliminating just one byte in a Note On message would mean a note event could be transmitted in 33% less time. Well, such a scheme does exist, and is used frequently in MIDI instruments and sequencers.

The technique for reducing the amount of MIDI data needed for transmitting Channel Voice Messages is called *running status*. For example, if a four-note chord is played on a keyboard, the MIDI messages generally would look like this:

Velocity

Note 1	Note 2	Note 3	Note 4
90-27-42	**90**-32-48	**90**-36-51	**90**-37-46

Status	Note Number

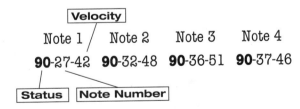

Figure 7-9
Polyphonic Key Pressure provides a different pressure value for each key.

The overall message consists of four consecutive Note On messages on MIDI Channel 1. It will take about four milliseconds to send this entire stream of information. Notice that the status message is the same for each note. It is a waste of time to resend the status byte for every data packet if the status is exactly the same for all of them. With running status, an instrument will *only send a status byte when the type of message changes*. Now this chord could be sent this way:

Note 1	Note 2	Note 3	Note 4
90-27-42	32-48	36-51	37-46

A status byte is sent at the beginning to define the type of data (Note On) and the channel (channel 1). Since the rest of the messages are also Note On events on channel 1, the status is *assumed* for all the remaining note messages by any receiving MIDI instruments. Running status has removed three messages from the message and saved a millisecond of time, which with a lot of MIDI data does add up.

There usually isn't a problem of speed when it's just one person playing a keyboard (unless you play more than 500 notes a second). Running status becomes important when a sequencer is simultaneously playing back many complex parts with large amounts of MIDI data. For this reason, sequencers will strip away all the unneeded status messages to create running status.

Note events are not the biggest time saver from using running status. There are rarely more than a few dozen notes in a measure of most music. However, moving a pitch bend wheel or using Aftertouch can send out hundreds of messages in a very short time. Here, running status becomes much more important. The savings in time add up to a big increase in efficiency.

MIDI was designed with the most demanding needs of musicians in mind. Running status is used to help achieve those goals. Best of all, you never have to think or worry about it, it all happens automatically. How many things can you say that about?

SUMMARY

These Channel Voice Messages, along with the Continuous Controllers described in the next chapter, are the basic musical components of MIDI. They form the building blocks of any musical performance. With Note On, Note Off, Pitch Bend Change, Channel Pressure, Polyphonic Key Pressure, and Program Change, a complex musical performance can be transmitted from one controlling instrument over a cable to any number of receiving instruments, which will instantly and accurately reproduce every nuance of the original. As you'll learn in detail later, that data can also be recorded, edited, layered and played back with a computer and special software, for unlimited creative potential.

Remember that each Channel Voice Message is transmitted on a single channel only. MIDI channels are selected on the transmitting instrument. All MIDI instruments have a channel selector control. The channel information for all MIDI Channel Voice Messages is contained within the bits of each status byte. Only those instruments set to the same channel as the sending instrument will respond to the information being received. Instruments connected to the sender but set to different channels still receive the data, but will ignore it. MIDI is capable of sending messages on many different channels all over a single cable, like watching one station on your cable television.

8

MIDI Controllers

In addition to the pitch bend wheel found on nearly all MIDI keyboards, there are other pedals, wheels, and levers used for controlling other expressive elements of a synthesizer's sound, such as vibrato, brightness, loudness and so forth. These pedals and wheels are referred to as *controllers*, since they allow you control over some part of a synthesizer's sound. As they are moved, each controller can cause the sound of the synthesizer to vary in some way. At the same time, they also send out MIDI data to indicate that the controller has been moved. Any synthesizer on the same channel as the sender will also vary its sound in some way.

Unlike the pressing of a key, which sends out only a single MIDI message, these wheels, sliders or levers send out large streams of MIDI information continuously whenever they are manipulated. The type of MIDI message sent out is called *Control Change*, also called *continuous controllers* because of the streams of data they often send. Each type of physical controller is represented by a unique *controller number*. When a physical controller is moved, the instrument sends a MIDI Control Change message as shown in **Figure 8-1**.

Instruments will respond to these messages in a variety of ways, some more obvious than others. Controllers such as the *modulation wheel* or *sustain*

pedal are more predictable in the effect they will have on a receiving synthesizer's sound—the first adds vibrato, while the second one allows a note to continue ringing even after you release the key, just like a piano. Other MIDI Control Change messages, such as the *breath controller* or *data entry* may not be as obvious in their effect on a sound, because the effect is individually programmable for each synthesizer patch, and not predetermined. Some controller numbers are not really connected with a specific physical wheel or pedal, but still have some modifying effect on a synthesizer's sound.

Many keyboards, in addition to a single pitch and modulation wheel, will have one or more programmable sliders, which can be set to send any desired Control Change message. There are also MIDI devices that are merely a set of sliders, each capable of sending any controller message on any MIDI channel.

Figure 8-2 is the current complete list of MIDI Controllers and the numbers assigned to them. New controller definitions are added to the list as the need for more control over a MIDI performance becomes necessary. A few brief explanations of some of the more important features of the controllers follow...

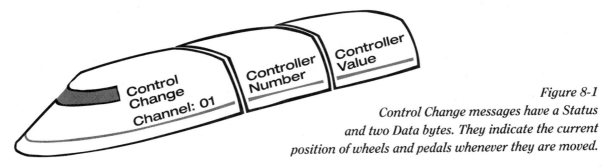

Figure 8-1
Control Change messages have a Status and two Data bytes. They indicate the current position of wheels and pedals whenever they are moved.

CTRL#	DEFINITION	CTRL#	DEFINITION
0	Bank Select	71	Sound Controller 2
1	Modulation wheel or lever		(default: Timbre/Harmonic Content)
2	Breath Controller	72	Sound Controller 3
3	Currently Undefined		(default: Release Time)
4	Foot controller	73	Sound Controller 4
5	Portamento time		(default: Attack Time)
6	Data entry MSB	74	Sound Controller 5
7	Main volume		(default: Brightness)
8	Balance	75-79	Sound Controllers 6-10 (no defaults)
9	Currently Undefined	80-83	General Purpose Controllers 5-8
10	Pan	84	Portamento Control
11	Expression Pedal	85-90	Currently Undefined
12	Effect Control 1	91	Effects 1 Depth
13	Effect Control 2	92	Effects 2 Depth
14-15	Currently Undefined	93	Effects 3 Depth
16-19	General Purpose Controllers 1-4	94	Effects 4 Depth
20-31	Currently Undefined	95	Effects 5 Depth
32-37	LSB for values 0-5	96	Data increment
38	Data Entry LSB	97	Data decrement
39-63	LSB for values 7-31	98	Non-Registered
64	Damper pedal (sustain)		Parameter Number LSB
65	Portamento On/Off	99	Non-Registered
66	Sostenuto		Parameter Number MSB
67	Soft pedal	100	Registered Parameter Number LSB
68	Legato Footswitch	101	Registered Parameter Number MSB
69	Hold 2	102-119	Currently Undefined
70	Sound Controller 1	120-127	Reserved for
	(default: Sound Variation)		Channel Mode Messages

Figure 8-1 MIDI Continuous Controllers.

#0 BANK SELECT

Program Change allows for 128 possible presets to be recalled on an instrument via MIDI. However, many MIDI instruments offer hundreds of presets. In order to access them from MIDI, most of these devices respond to Bank Select, which functions as a sort of extension to Program Change. By sending a Bank Select along with a bank number, followed by a Program Change command (either from a special patch button found on a master keyboard controller or a programmed into a sequencer), MIDI can access over 16,000 patches on any MIDI channel.

#1 MODULATION WHEEL

This common controller is found on virtually all MIDI instruments. It is a wheel or lever that, when moved, adds *modulation* to a sound. The musical term for modulation is *vibrato*, an essential element of musical expression. Modulation can be used to create pitch vibrato (frequency modulation), loudness vibrato (amplitude modulation), brightness vibrato (filter modulation), or for some special digital effects on cer-

tain instruments. The effect that the modulation wheel has on a particular sound is decided by the synthesizer's patch, and is not defined directly in MIDI.

#2 BREATH CONTROLLER

The *breath controller* was introduced by Yamaha for the DX7, a popular early MIDI digital synthesizer. It is used most often for exactly the same functions as the modulation wheel, but instead of a wheel you move with your hands, it's a device you place in your mouth and blow into. Blowing harder produces higher MIDI controller values. While other companies never made a breath controller, their instruments can respond to its MIDI controller number and use it for some sort of modulation.

#3 FOOT CONTROLLER

The *foot controller* is a universal control that can perform any one of a number of functions. It is created mainly by a special pedal that operates like the gas pedal of a car. It sends a continuous stream of values depending on how you move your foot. Like the breath controller or the modulation wheel it can be used for vibrato, brightness, etc.

#7 VOLUME

This message controls an instrument's audio output level, much like turning the volume up or down on a radio. This is perhaps one of the most important controllers in the list. With MIDI Volume, you can "mix" the levels on all your instruments without touching them. It can also be used to change levels during a performance, or within a sequence. MIDI Volume does for synthesizers what costly mixing automation does in the most expensive recording studios.

While virtually all instruments respond to Controller #7, few have an actual slider or knob to send this parameter. Some instruments have user programmable sliders, one of which can be set to send MIDI Volume. The volume knob on the front panel of an instrument does not send MIDI volume data.

#10 PAN

Pan is short for *panorama*. In audio, this is the ability to move a sound in stereo "field," meaning left or right between the speakers. Most synthesizers provide a stereo audio output, with the sound coming from both sides of the output. By sending MIDI Pan messages to an instrument, the current sound will appear to move from the left speaker (Pan=0) to the right speaker (Pan=127). Multi-timbral instruments have several instruments, all coming out of the same stereo audio outputs. MIDI Pan can be used to set and move any instrument left or right from the outputs.

#32 - #37
LEAST SIGNIFICANT BYTE (LSB)

As mentioned earlier, the Pitch Bend message in MIDI uses two bytes of data instead of one to increase the number of possible values, and thus give smoother control over the pitch changes. A single MIDI data byte can only be a value from 0 to 127. By combining it with a second data byte, a data message can now express over 16,000 different values.

Some instruments are designed to send certain controllers using two bytes for the value, if more precise resolution is desired. When a single byte is used, it is called the *Most Significant Byte (MSB)*. The second byte sent is the LSB, the Least Significant Byte. They are sent separately, so each of these LSB messages is preceded by its own status message and controller number. LSB codes are not used often.

#64 SUSTAIN PEDAL

Pianos have three pedals—a *damper* pedal, a *soft* pedal, and a *sostenuto* pedal. These are all used in MIDI, and each has its own controller number. The most common of these is Controller 64–*sustain*. It works just like a piano's sustain pedal, allowing notes to continue sounding even after the keys have been released.

#91 - 95 EFFECTS DEPTH

These are used to control external sound processing effects through the use of a MIDI-controlled audio effects loop on a mixer or amplifier. Many synthesizers have built-in digital effects, and these too can be controlled by these five messages. Effects Depth messages can be sent from a programmable MIDI data slider.

#98 - 101 NON-REGISTERED
AND REGISTERED PARAMETERS

While MIDI is not primarily intended to control the timbre of an instrument directly during a performance, this feature is available from some instruments. Specific types of "universal" controls—such as filter cutoff, envelope rates, or pitch bend range—have been assigned *parameter numbers* and can send their current position when changed by a front panel knob or slider. These are used by instruments with extra controls, such as joysticks or front panel sliders. The currently defined Registered Parameters list is:

01	Pitch Bend Sensitivity
02	Fine Tuning
03	Coarse Tuning

As with the other MIDI channel voice messages, Control Change data is sent on a single MIDI channel. Instruments set to the same channel as the sender will respond. Further, not all controller numbers are recognized in any one instrument. A receiving instrument will simply ignore messages for the controllers it can not recognize. The amount of modulation that any controller will have on a particular synthesizer parameter is programmed on the individual synthesizer.

The list of controller numbers goes from #0 to #120. The controller numbers from 121 to 127 are reserved for a very different type of function called a *Mode Message*. These can make a synthesizer change its response to MIDI data. The next chapter deals with these messages in greater detail.

9

Channel Mode Messages

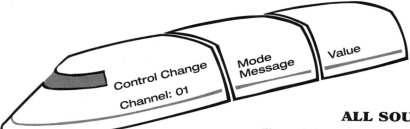

*Figure 9-1
Mode messages change
how an instrument responds to
other MIDI commands.*

The MIDI messages you've seen thus far communicate all the elements of a performance from a master instrument to other slave instruments. They either command an instrument to play a sound, or add some expressive component to it. The Channel Mode messages are a group of special Controller messages that alter the way a synthesizer responds to other MIDI events or commands. Here is a list of the Channel Mode Messages:

ALL SOUND OFF

This message acts as a sort of MIDI panic button. It commands the instruments on the same channel to stop all notes immediately. This command may be sent automatically by sequencer when it is stopped, in order to silence any sustained notes. It would also shut off all the lights on a MIDI lighting console, or silence a MIDI-controlled reverb or delay effects unit.

RESET ALL CONTROLLERS

When an instrument receives this message on the same channel to which it is set, it will set all of its continuous controllers back to an ideal initial condition. This means that the sustain pedal will be up, the modulation wheel will be at zero, the pitch bend will be off, there will be no Aftertouch currently in play, and so forth. Like the All Sound Off command, it is used primarily by a sequencer when it is stopped in the middle of a song.

CHANNEL MODE MESSAGES

MESSAGE	CONTROL NUMBER	ADDITIONAL DATA
All Sound Off	120	None
Reset All Controllers	121	None
Local Control	122	(On /Off)
All Notes Off	123	None
Omni Mode Off	124	None
Omni Mode On	125	None
Mono Mode On	126	Number of channels (1 to 16)
Poly Mode On	127	None

LOCAL CONTROL

A keyboard synthesizer has two distinct parts: the keyboard itself and the synthesizer that actually produces the sounds. When played, the keyboard trig-

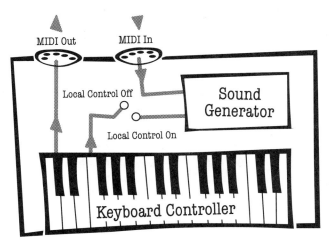

Figure 9-2
The Local Control Mode message separates a MIDI instrument's keyboard from its own sound generator.

gers the synthesizer *and* sends out MIDI messages. The Local Control message, when followed by a data message of 0 (off), electronically disconnects the two. This is called *Local Control Off*. In this mode, the keyboard continues to send data when played, but it no longer triggers sounds from its own synthesizer. At the same time, the synthesizer section will continue to respond to incoming MIDI messages while ignoring the attached keyboard. The keyboard can send on one MIDI channel, while the synthesizer responds to another. This is especially important for sequencing, when only the sequencer should be triggering the synthesizer while you play in new parts for other instruments in the studio. Local Control can be set either from an instrument's front panel or via an incoming MIDI message. A local Control Message followed by a data message of 1 (on) will reconnect the keyboard to its resident synthesizer. This is *Local Control On*.

ALL NOTES OFF

This message is very close to the All Sound Off message described above. It functions as a MIDI panic button to stop the sounds currently playing. It is usually sent automatically by a sequencer upon stopping PLAY. It is sometimes found on MIDI patchbays as a Panic button which you can press in the event of a stuck note on a synthesizer. The All Notes Off command differs in a couple of ways. First, it only stops notes – not affecting lighting systems or other non-

musical devices. Secondly, it only shuts off notes triggered by MIDI, and not notes being played manually on a synthesizer's own keyboard.

MIDI MODES

The second four messages are quite different. These change the basic way in which an instrument responds to incoming MIDI data. Modes have the most use for those people using non-keyboard electronic instruments such as MIDI guitarists and MIDI woodwind players.

There are two categories of MIDI modes, *Omni* and *Poly*, which can be combined four different ways.

Mode 1 — Omni On / Poly
Mode 2 — Omni On / Mono
Mode 3 — Omni Off / Poly
Mode 4 — Omni Off / Mono

The Omni (meaning "all") modes determine whether a synthesizer will respond to incoming data on an individual MIDI channel or to data on *any* channel. In *Omni On* mode, a receiving instrument will play all incoming MIDI information, regardless of the MIDI channel. In *Omni Off* mode, an instrument responds only to information on the single channel to which it is set, which is called an instrument's *basic channel*.

MODE 3: OMNI OFF / POLY

The most common MIDI mode is Mode 3: Omni Off / Poly, which makes a synthesizer respond to incoming MIDI information on a single MIDI channel. Single timbre synthesizers, when set to a desired MIDI channel, only respond to MIDI messages received on that channel. Any messages received on the other 15 channels are simply ignored. Multitimbral instruments can respond to MIDI information on several channels at once. They operate just as if they were several separate instruments, but all in a single box. Each "slot" in the multitimbral instrument responds to its one MIDI channel. Multitimbral instruments also have a basic channel for sending MIDI or receiving certain voice messages such as a global patch change or for System Exclusive messages. MIDI channels are set by you on the instrument itself. *There is no command in MIDI to tell an instrument to change its MIDI channel.*

MODE 1: OMNI ON / POLY

In this mode, a synthesizer will play MIDI data received from *any* MIDI channel, and will play in a normal, polyphonic way. It is rarely used, but is available on most instruments. This mode is fine for layering or combining the sounds of many synthesizers, especially on stage. However, you are better off simply setting all your instruments to a single channel, since later this mode can cause confusion when you use a sequencer, and you want each synthesizer to respond to only the MIDI channel to which it is set.

MODE 4 : OMNI OFF / MONO

This mode is most often used by MIDI guitarists. A MIDI guitar controller is different than a keyboard controller in that each string can have unique properties. Guitarists may bend a note on one or two strings while leaving the others alone. They may also want to have a bass timbre for the bottom string and other timbres for the higher strings. With a keyboard controller, the machine doesn't know which finger is pressing any given key, but a guitar is like six separate controllers, each playing a single note. It is possible, for example, to have a MIDI guitar controller send on six different MIDI channels so that each string can send an individual pitch bend on its own MIDI channel.

When a MIDI instrument is put into *Omni Off/Mono* mode, it is effectively divided up into a number of monophonic instruments. Included in the

Guitar synthesizers take full advantage of MIDI modes!

mode message is the number of monophonic voices desired. For a guitarist, this would be six, the same number of strings on their MIDI guitar controller. Any number of voices can be specified, but it is limited by the number of voices available in the instrument or 16, which ever is smaller. In this mode, each voice of the instrument will respond to a different MIDI channel, can only play a single note at a time, and can usually be set to a separate timbre.

For example, a synthesizer on MIDI channel 4 (the instrument's *basic channel*) set to Omni Off/Mono mode, and six voices will respond to the channels 4, 5, 6, 7, 8, and 9. Each voice of the synthesizer takes its own MIDI channel and plays monophonically. What makes this different from the more standard Poly mode is that each voice can have individual pitch bend, MIDI volume, or Aftertouch. If the instrument is multitimbral, each voice can play with a different preset sound as well. In poly mode, a pitch bend or other controller would affect all the notes being played on that channel.

MODE 2 : OMNI ON / MONO

This mode is the least useful, and also least used of the four MIDI modes. A synthesizer will accept messages from any channel (Omni), but it becomes just like a monophonic synthesizer, never playing more than one note at a time. This mode was not part of the original MIDI specification, but a major manufacturer misunderstood Mode 4 and put this on a very popular synthesizer by mistake. This extra mode was added to accommodate the situation, but has never been implemented since.

SETTING MODES

A synthesizer's mode may be changed either on its front panel or by receiving a command over MIDI. Instruments respond to Mode change messages on their basic channel, and will stop playing all current notes at the time of the change (like receiving an All Notes Off message).

These modes are descriptions only of how a synthesizer will *receive* a MIDI message. MIDI controllers do not *send* data in Omni Off or Omni On. All Channel Messages are always sent on a single channel. A sending instrument could, however, be Mono or Poly.

The four available modes for MIDI instruments add versatility to certain MIDI systems. Most MIDI musicians will never encounter modes other than Omni Off/Poly, but we can all sleep better knowing they are there.

Real Time Messages

MIDI sequencers and drum machines record MIDI data and play it back, just like a multitrack tape recorder. These devices have built-in timers, called *clocks,* to specify and maintain a tempo. In order to get two or more devices to synchronize their performances, their clocks must be set to exactly the same speed. Before MIDI, it was quite a chore to synchronize a sequencer to a drum machine or to another sequencer. Imagine trying to get two tape recorders, each with the same music in them to play together perfectly. Not only would they have to run at precisely the same speed (rare), but you would have to trigger them at the exact same moment. Go ahead, try. I DARE YOU! (Okay, you can stop trying, I think you got my point.)

Part of the reason for such problems in connecting MIDI sequencers is in the different ways the clocks in them have been implemented. Like snowflakes, no two are exactly the same, though they may look (or in this case sound) like it.

In order for a MIDI sequencer to record and reproduce a performance accurately, it must time incoming musical events accurately. It does it by measuring the time in between each incoming MIDI event. A tempo is set on a sequencer measured in *beats per minute* (BPM). Internally, however, the sequencer divides each beat into a number of much smaller parts (**Figure 10-1**).

Just as a musical metronome using BPM divides a minute into a specific number of beats, a sequencer divides a beat into a specific number of clock *ticks*. There are a few names given to these sequencer clock ticks: *timebase, clock rate, resolution,* or *PPQN* (*parts per quarter note*). They all mean the same thing, that time is being broken down and measured in small fractions of time based on the tempo. Time is measured by counting the clock ticks between MIDI events. At each tick, a sequencer checks the MIDI IN port to see if any messages have come in.

If there is no incoming data, the sequencer merely adds to the count of the clock ticks and keeps looking. Whenever a MIDI message enters the sequencer from a transmitting MIDI instrument, the sequencer will record it along with the current clock tick number (**Figure 10-2**). When the sequencer is playing back MIDI data, it will use the same clock tick number to know just when to play the recorded message.

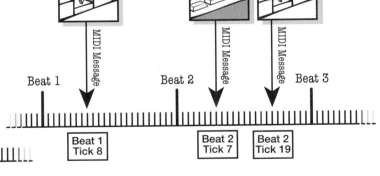

Figure 10-2
The time between beats is measured by a MIDI sequencer whenever a new message arrives.

Beat 1   Beat 2   Beat 3

Clock Ticks

Figure 10-1
MIDI divides each beat into 24 parts with clock messages.

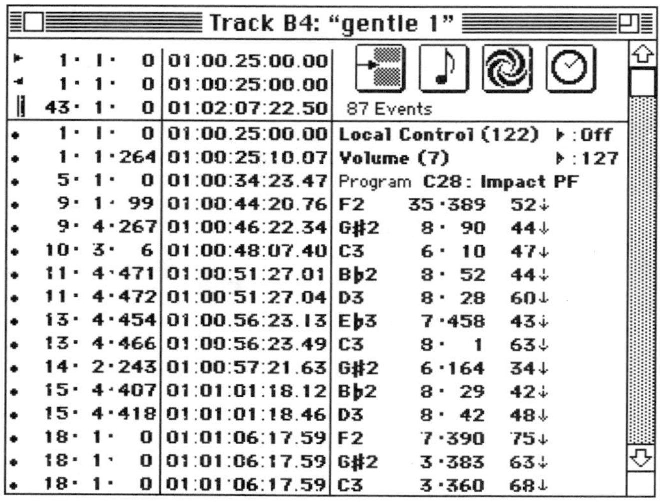

▣▣ ▓▓▓▓▓▓ Track B4: "gentle 1" ▓▓▓▓▓ ▣▣	
► 1·1· 0	01:00.25.00.00
◄ 1·1· 0	01:00.25.00.00
‖ 43·1· 0	01:02:07.22.50

• 1·1· 0	01:00.25.00.00	Local Control (122) ►:Off
• 1·1·264	01:00.25.10.07	Volume (7) ►:127
• 5·1· 0	01:00.34.23.47	Program C28: Impact PF
• 9·1·99	01:00.44.20.76	F2 35·389 52↓
• 9·4·267	01:00.46.22.34	G♯2 8· 90 44↓
• 10·3· 6	01:00.48:07.40	C3 6· 10 47↓
• 11·4·471	01:00.51.27.01	B♭2 8· 52 44↓
• 11·4·472	01:00.51.27.04	D3 8· 28 60↓
• 13·4·454	01:00.56.23.13	E♭3 7·458 43↓
• 13·4·466	01:00.56.23.49	C3 8· 1 63↓
• 14·2·243	01:00.57.21.63	G♯2 6·164 34↓
• 15·4·407	01:01.01.18.12	B♭2 8· 29 42↓
• 15·4·418	01:01.01.18.46	D3 8· 42 48↓
• 18·1· 0	01:01.06.17.59	F2 7·390 75↓
• 18·1· 0	01:01.06.17.59	G♯2 3·383 63↓
• 18·1· 0	01:01.06.17.59	C3 3·360 68↓

Figure 10-3
*The MIDI Event Editor of a computer-based
sequencer. Note that each event has a time and
duration displayed.*

SYSTEM REAL TIME MESSAGES

DEFINITION	DATA BYTES
Timing Clock	(none)
Undefined	(none)
Start	(none)
Continue	(none)
Stop	(none)
Active Sensing	(none)
System Reset	(none)

A sequencer will always use the same number of clock ticks for each beat. Sequencers with higher resolutions (more clock ticks for each beat) record more accurately the rhythms and timing nuances of a musical performance transmitted over MIDI. Drum machines and sequencers vary in their timing resolution, and thus their accuracy.

GETTING IN SYNC

It would be almost impossible for two devices, such as a sequencer and a drum machine to synchronize, if each used its own internal timing clock. In order for two machines to synchronize, they must share a single clock to command them when to start and how fast to go. The timing clock in one machine acts as a *master* and provides clocking to the other devices, known as *slaves*. Before MIDI, different machines—both drum machines and sequencers—used different timebases for their clocks. Some used 24 PPQN, while others used 48 or 96 PPQN. Plus, instruments used various kinds of connectors and electrical impulses, making them more difficult or impossible to interconnect.

One of MIDI's goals is to remove incompatibilities between musical instruments, including the clock-based ones. Instead of using simple electrical pulses, as found in earlier clock-based instruments, MIDI uses special codes to synchronize instruments from any manufacturer. These codes are called *System Real Time* messages. Here is a complete list of them:

MIDI uses a timebase of 24. That is, 24 times per beat (based on the tempo of the master instrument) a MIDI sequencer or drum machine will send out the *Timing Clock* code for synchronization through its MIDI OUT port. The Timing Clock, like all Real Time messages, has no channel; it is used to address all the instruments in a MIDI system. Instruments that do not use clocks, such as ordinary synthesizers, simply ignore the incoming clock messages.

MIDI sequencers and drum machines have resolutions much higher than 24 ticks per beat. The MIDI Timing Clock message doesn't actually replace a sequencer's internal clock, instead it continuously *corrects* the slave's clock to keep perfect time with the master. Thus MIDI can synchronize any device, regardless of its resolution. All devices in a MIDI system will always play exactly together. Tempo can change anytime during the playback of music by slowing down the rate that the Timing Clocks are sent out. The same 24-clock messages are sent each beat, but now the beats are slower and further apart.

In addition to the Timing Clock, there are other MIDI Real Time messages used for starting and stopping the music. When you press the PLAY button on your sequencer, the MIDI *Start* message is sent to command all other clock-based devices to begin playing from the beginning of the song currently selected in their memory. They will play at the tempo being sent by the master. When you press STOP on your sequencer, the MIDI *Stop* message is sent by the master to command all the synchronized devices to immediately stop playing.

All sequencers have the option of playing from some point other than the beginning of the song. The MIDI Start message always means "play from the beginning." In order to start from somewhere in the middle, MIDI has another message called *Continue*. It is used in a manner similar to Start. However, it signals the slaved devices to begin playing at whatever point the sequencer last stopped.

As an example, consider a MIDI system with a master keyboard synthesizer, a sequencer and a drum machine.

- MIDI Out from the keyboard goes to the sequencer in order to record the performance.

- MIDI OUT from the sequencer is connected to MIDI IN of the drum machine and the synthesizer (some sequencers have multiple MIDI Outs, for other ways to do this see *Chapter 17*).

- Your performance on the synthesizer's keyboard is recorded into the sequencer.

- A drum part you have created for the same song is stored in the drum machine's memory.

- You want to play back the music in the sequencer and have the drum machine play along in sync.

Figure 10-4 illustrates a typical, simple MIDI system setup.

All MIDI sequencers and drum machines have a synchronization option with *internal* and *external* sync. *Internal sync* makes a device a master, with its own timing clock to determine the tempo. In the *external sync* mode (called *MIDI sync* on some devices), an instrument uses the Timing Clocks from a master device elsewhere in the system to determine the tempo at which it records and plays. In this example, the sequencer is set to internal sync mode and the drum machine is set to external sync.

When devices that send MIDI Clock aren't playing, they continue to send out Timing Clocks. Doing so helps prepare all slave devices to play at the exact tempo, even from the first moment. If Clocks weren't sent out, it would take the slave a few moments to lock up to the master, during which time their playback could be erratic.

When you press the START button on your sequencer, a MIDI Start byte is sent between two of the Timing Clocks and signals the drum machine to begin at the same time it does. The two machines run in exact synchronization from that moment on. When you press STOP on the sequencer, both units will cease playing. Pressing CONTINUE on the sequencer will make both units start from the point at which they were stopped. Pressing START will start both machines from the first measure of the song again.

If this example of using MIDI Real Time with a sequencer and drum machine seems rather simple, that's because it is. The basic idea to remember in any MIDI system is that one clock-based device acts as the master, while all the rest are slaves. Real Time messages are sent along with all other MIDI Channel and Controller messages. A separate cable is not needed for Real Time information. It is possible to use the MIDI THRU of a synthesizer to connect a drum machine, if your sequencer has only one MIDI OUT.

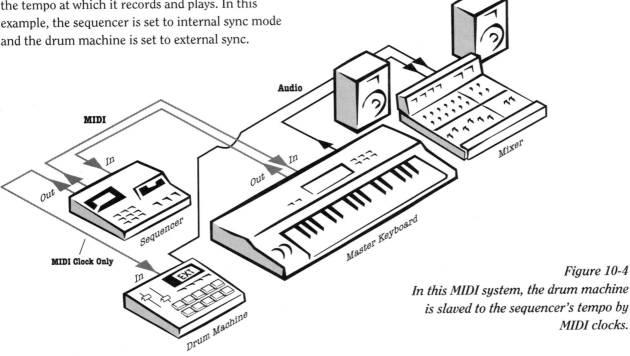

Figure 10-4
In this MIDI system, the drum machine is slaved to the sequencer's tempo by MIDI clocks.

Figure 10-5
This setup will function exactly the same
*as the one in **Figure 10-4**.*

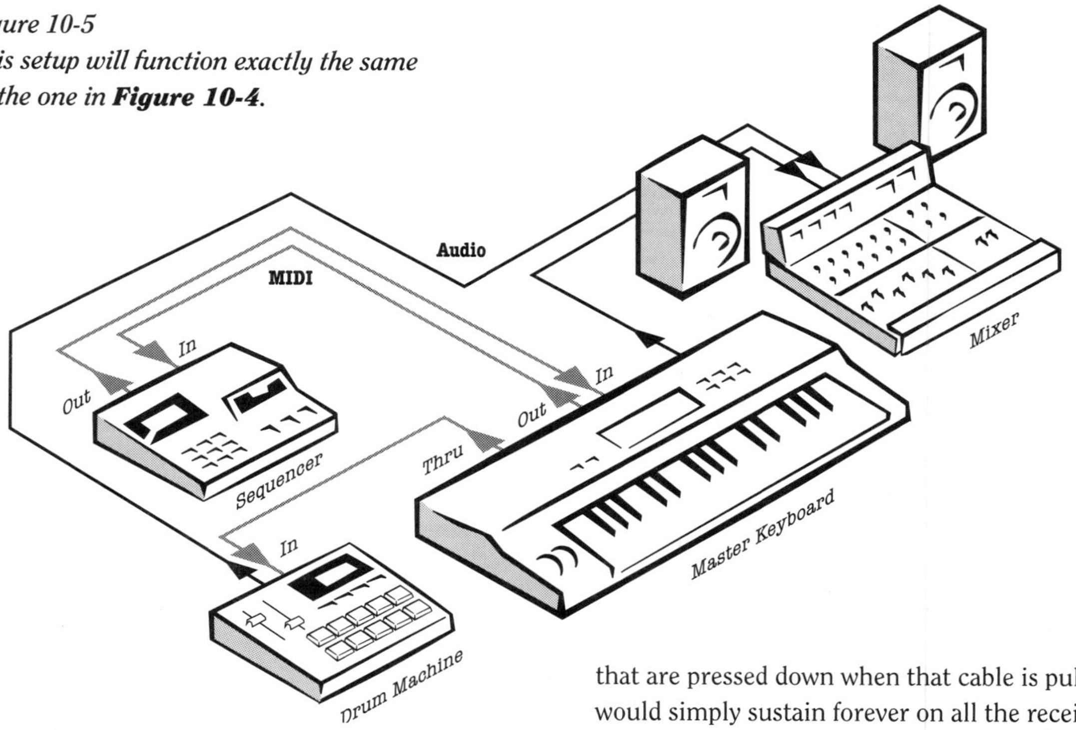

In addition to sequencers and drum machines, there are also some MIDI-controlled digital effects processors that can recognize Timing Clock. For example, many such processors can lock a Digital Delay to MIDI Clock. This provides echoes that stay in time to the music. There are also MIDI-compatible metronomes to provide clicks to musicians who rely on MIDI Real Time messages to function.

The popularity of keyboard workstations has grown enormously as the quality of these combination keyboard controller, synthesizer, sequencer, drum machine and effects processors has improved. With everything under one roof, there is no need to think about synchronization of separate machines, it all happens in one place. The same is true of musicians using samplers and drum sound modules along with their standard sequencer instead of using a drum machine; the need to use MIDI Real Time diminishes.

There is more to synchronization than just Timing Clocks, Start, Stop and Continue. Later you'll see ways to synchronize sequencers with audio and video tape recorders.

ACTIVE SENSING

What would happen if one of the MIDI cables in your system was accidentally unplugged while you were performing or playing a sequence? While there is no harm to instruments by plugging and unplugging MIDI cables with the power on, there would be a rather disastrous effect on your music. Any notes

that are pressed down when that cable is pulled would simply sustain forever on all the receiving instruments. Any drum machines synchronized to the sequencer would grind to a halt. Not a good thing if your hoping to do an encore.

Because MIDI only travels in one direction in a MIDI cable, a transmitting controller is never aware of whether its signal is being received or not by other instruments. A function in MIDI called *Active Sensing* is implemented on many instruments to ensure that there will be no "hanging" notes or other problems in the event of a lost connection. The Active Sensing message is a single byte sent about three times every second (every 300 milliseconds to be exact) when no other MIDI data is being sent. Once an instrument begins to receive the Active Sensing message, it will expect to continue receiving data at least 3 times a second. If no MIDI messages of any kind are received after a period of time, the instrument will assume that there is a problem (someone tripped over a cable, or a jealous member of another band pulled it out), and will simply shut down, turning off all notes playing at the time. This is most useful for on-stage performing, where accidents can and do happen at the worst, most embarrassing times (such as when people are in the audience).

SYSTEM RESET

In the manual of practically every MIDI instrument, you can find a description of how that instrument behaves when it is first turned on. Some instruments will be in Omni On/Poly while others will be Omni Off/Poly. Some instruments can be set to ignore or recognize Aftertouch, Volume or other MIDI controllers. Many of these parameters can be changed through MIDI or from the front panel so the instrument functions quite differently. The *System Reset* message commands a receiving instrument to go back to the state it was in when first turned on. This message has no MIDI channel, so it will affect *all* the instruments connected to the sender. It is included as a Real Time message because it is usually sent only by sequencers, not synthesizers.

MIDI TIME CODE (MTC)

Synthesizers and sequencers are vital tools in film and video scoring and production as both musical instruments and sound-effects generators. MIDI samplers give movie sound effects designers new palettes of interesting, unique and bizarre sounds. The extensive use of sequencers by composers in film and video scoring has created a new set of needs for synchronization. In the case of sound effects, a sound like a gunshot or door slam must be triggered at just the right moment to match the picture. Writing film music has very special requirements. A section of music—called a *cue*—must begin and end at very precise moments in the picture. The process of scoring to picture involves synchronizing a sequencer and a video tape machine (VCR).

MIDI Real Time messages coordinate the playback of multiple MIDI devices, ensuring that they run at the same tempo and are synchronized. However, the standard Real Time messages are not enough to handle the special needs of film and video work. While Real Time messages are *tempo-oriented*, film and video are *event-oriented*.

MIDI Time Code, or MTC, is a MIDI function that links MIDI—the standard of the music world—to *SMPTE Time Code*, the standard for synchronization in the film and video world. SMPTE stands for *Society of Motion Picture and Television Engineers*. It is the technical standards organization that developed the techniques used for film and video synchronization. They developed a technology called *SMPTE time code*, which is a sophisticated system used throughout the world for synchronizing video and audio equipment.

Time code is a special audio signal put onto both audio and video tapes. Contained in the audio signal is a digital code with numbers that can be read and recognized by special synchronization equipment connected to the audio output of those machines. When a tape containing SMPTE time code is played, the code goes out to the synchronizers, which read the numbers and use them to coordinate other equipment. SMPTE time code is used for locking an audio tape machine to a video tape machine, and MIDI sequencers as well.

The numbers encoded in SMPTE time code do not have a tempo value, like MIDI Real Time Clock messages. Instead they refer to specific points in *real time*. Real time is just like the clock on the wall, calibrated in hours, minutes and seconds. SMPTE time code is the same: it stamps a unique number on every moment of a tape with an hour, minute, second and *frame*. When the code on a tape is played, any other device in the system can know the exact position of the tape currently playing and, with the proper synchronization equipment, adjust its own speed to match it. Because of its use in video production, SMPTE time code is accurate down to the *frame*.

Video tape in the U.S. and many other countries around the world run at a speed of thirty frames per second. Thus time code is accurate to 1/30th of a second. In Europe, video runs at 25 frames per second, and the time code used there (called *EBU code*) matches that. Though SMPTE time code was designed initially for video machine synchronization, it is used routinely for audio recording studio applications.

MTC works by reading time code from an audio or video tape, through a *SMPTE to MTC converter*. These converters can either be a stand-alone box, or built into a sequencer or computer MIDI interface. As time code is read from a tape, the converter sends the current hour, minute, second, and frame number in MIDI format to a MIDI sequencer or computer program designed to read the MTC messages. The sequencer is given a specific time code number to begin playback, and holds the music's tempo or tempos.

The basic MTC message indicates the current position of the audio or video tape, and is sent four times every frame (120 times per second) in the following format:

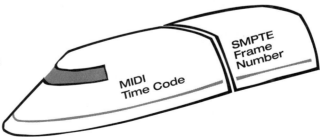

Figure 10-6
The MIDI Time Code message
indicates the current tape position.

Most musicians will use SMPTE time code and MTC to lock a sequencer to audio or video tape. But MTC has another function for those people in film sound effects, live theater production and some other special applications. Events such as triggering a sound effect with a sampler, starting or stopping a sequencer or drum machine remotely, or even adjusting stage lights or video cameras can be automatically activated using a special *MIDI System Exclusive* code designed for use with MTC.

An MTC *Event List* is a numbered list of events and the SMPTE time that each should occur. The list can be generated by a specialized MTC computer program and sent to MTC devices and other MIDI instruments, indicating when events should be triggered and the nature of the events (play a note, record on a track of tape, etc.). The Event List is sent out ahead of time in order to program compatible synchronizers, tape machines, lighting consoles or other special devices with the events and their times. The specialized MTC sequencer receives SMPTE time code from some source, such as a video tape. Whenever an event is just about to happen, another System Exclusive message is sent out to all the

devices in the system signaling that it is time to trigger the next event in the list. The basic MTC position message is sent in between events to keep all the MTC devices synchronized and ready.

While special MTC compatible machines exist, computers with MIDI interfaces are the primary tools for use with MTC. MTC is usually not transmitted over the same cable of a MIDI system as Channel Voice Messages. This helps prevent a MIDI "logjam" from occurring, since the MTC message is sent so often. **Figure 10-7** illustrates an example of a basic MTC music sequencing setup for scoring to picture.

SUMMARY

MIDI Time Code and the other System Real Time commands bring the world of MIDI sequencers and drum machines into the world of multitrack tape recorders and video tape, and ensure perfect synchronization. Much of MIDI is geared toward allowing a single master instrument or device to have complete control over an entire MIDI system. The Real Time commands maintain that idea for the more complex needs of the recording musician.

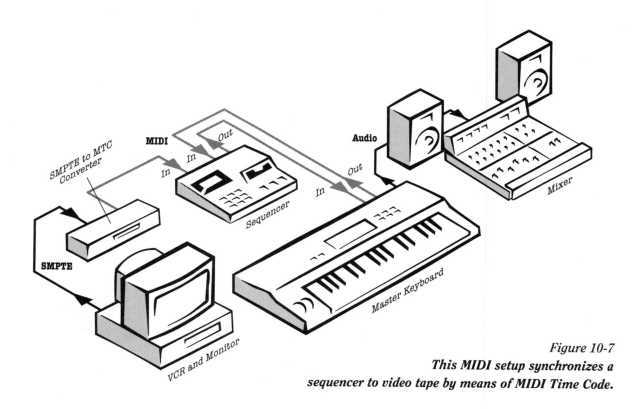

Figure 10-7
This MIDI setup synchronizes a sequencer to video tape by means of MIDI Time Code.

11

System Common Messages

There are a small number of MIDI messages that are used to support other MIDI functions and make no sound on their own. They are called *System Common Messages*. These messages help increase the power and usefulness of MIDI music systems that include sequencers, drum machines, computers and older synthesizers.

SONG POSITION POINTER

When a *Start* command is sent through MIDI, all clock-based instruments start playing from the beginning of the song programmed in their memory. If they are sent a *Stop* while playing, they will cease playing, hold their place in the music, and will play from that point if sent the *Continue* command.

Professional multitrack tape recorders have the ability to find specific points on a tape and play them. This function—*autolocating*—makes it much easier to fix or add something to the middle of a recording. You certainly wouldn't want to start at the beginning of a long song each time you wanted to hear the ending. MIDI sequencers and drum machines all have the ability to *autolocate* by starting from a point other than the beginning of a song. It adds ease and power to a MIDI recording system, and saves a lot of time.

However, if you have a drum machine connected to your sequencer and you wish to record a part from bar 32, you would need to set the bar number on the sequencer, set the bar number on the drum machine, put the drum machine into MIDI sync mode, and *then* press Start on the sequencer. It would be necessary to do this every time you wanted to record or listen to that section of the music.

Fortunately, MIDI takes care of this chore for you with its *Song Position Pointer* command. Song Position Pointer is used in conjunction with System Real Time messages, the ones that link and synchronize the clocks in drum machines and sequencers linked in a system. It works like a MIDI autolocator. When a sequencer or drum machine is set to play from a certain measure, it will send this information out so that other clocked devices can also move to that same measure. When the machines are started by pressing Start on the master, a MIDI Continue message is sent and everything will begin from that exact point. Song Position Pointer could be compared to the conductor of an orchestra calling out a bar number for all the musicians to begin playing from, raising the baton, and then starting the music.

When set a playback location other than measure 1 on a sequencer or drum machine, the Song Position Pointer message is sent out. The value that is sent is the *number of sixteenth notes from the start of the piece* to the desired location. Any other sequencer or drum machine that is connected to the master, and is set to MIDI Sync mode, will respond by moving up in its own memory to the same location. When Start is pressed on the master, the System Real Time *Continue* message is sent out and every machine will start from the same location.

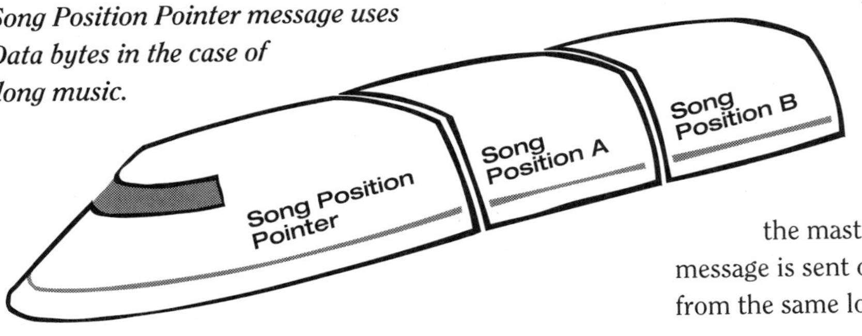

Figure 11–1
The Song Position Pointer message uses two Data bytes in the case of very long music.

SONG SELECT

In a situation where you have several pieces of music stored into both a separate sequencer and drum machine, it is handy to be able to choose a song on one machine and have the other machine in the system play that same choice. In fact, sequencers and drum machines that are able to store many pieces of music can do just that with the MIDI *Song Select* message.

Figure 11–2
The Song Select message allows separate sequencers and drum machines to play the same programmed music.

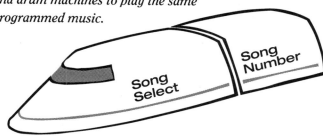

You can recall any song in a sequencer by a few button presses on the machine's front panel. As you do so, the sequencer will send out the Song Select message that commands all other machines to call up the same piece. However, just like Program Changes, you must be sure that you have placed the same song into each memory of each device: Song 1 must be in memory 1 of each machine, Song 2 must be in memory 2, etc. Song Select only sends the number of a song memory location. Whatever is in that location will play when a Real Time Start message is sent.

TUNE REQUEST

A problem with older analog synthesizers, unlike the digital instruments of today, is that they drift slowly out of tune over a period of time. After a while, the instrument needs retuning. The more sophisticated analog synthesizers included a special Tune button on their front panels, which would trigger an elec-

Figure 11–3
Tune Request keeps older analog synthesizers in tune.

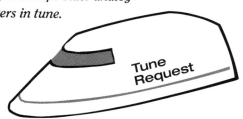

tronic "tuner" in the instrument to automatically retune each oscillator (the actual sound-producing hardware) to be in perfect tune with each other. The problem was the need to reach over to the instrument to hit the Tune button occasionally in order to stay in tune.

Those great-sounding, older synthesizers can be commanded to retune their oscillators automatically by sending the System Common *Tune Request* message. This accomplishes the same task as you pushing the Tune button on the instrument. For example, this command is useful if you place a Tune Request into a sequencer track during a moment of rest (tuning can take a few seconds), so an analog synthesizer can retune during that time. By their nature, digital synthesizers do not need, and will not respond to, Tune Request.

END OF SYSTEM EXCLUSIVE

The final System Common message is the *End Of System Exclusive* message. This tells all receiving instruments that a System Exclusive message, such as a memory dump from a synthesizer or sampler, is finished. For more details see *Chapter 12* on *System Exclusive* and its use.

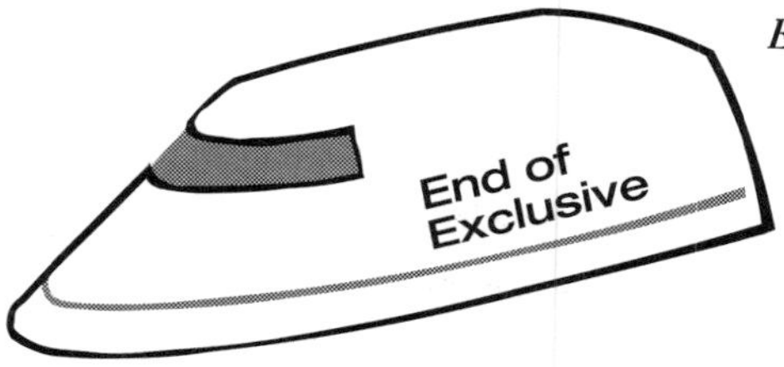

Figure 11–4
The End of Exclusive message is found at the end of every System Exclusive message.

SUMMARY

There is still room in the MIDI specification for more System Common messages if a new need arises. In general, System Common messages are used to augment the other types of MIDI messages, and are not complete by themselves. They don't make noises.

12

The Mysteries of System Exclusive

The MIDI messages you've learned about to this point all communicate information that is common among all electronic musical instruments. Regardless of whether an instrument produces sound by analog, digital, sampling, or a hybrid of technologies, all MIDI instruments are familiar with the notion of playing notes, bending pitch with a wheel, adding expressive modulation, pressing pedals, changing their program, and so forth. All MIDI sequencers and drum machines lock together, match their tempos, and start and stop as one. MIDI is the common language spoken by synthesizers of every make, model and price—the technological "melting pot."

System Exclusive messages are different. They are used for exchanging information that is *unique* to one particular instrument, and for transmitting special non-music, event-oriented information. There are three types of System Exclusive Messages:

- System Exclusive (with manufacturer ID numbers)

- Universal System Exclusive (Non-Real Time)

- Universal System Exclusive (Real Time)

Manufacturers of MIDI instruments use the first type of System Exclusive (or *Sysex* for short) message mainly to provide *access to the contents of an instrument's memory*. This is in contrast to what happens when pressing a program or patch button on a synthesizer to recall a patch. MIDI Program Change messages send only the number of the memory location, not the data of the patch itself.

System Exclusive encapsulates the actual parameter data of a single patch or the entire memory of an instrument and sends it via the MIDI OUT port. When another instrument of the same make and model receives the data, it is recognized as being the same type of data it uses, and stores it in its own memory. The receiving instrument now has the same patch information and will produce the same sounds. Sysex data can be transmitted between two of the same type of instrument, or, more importantly, between an instrument and a computer.

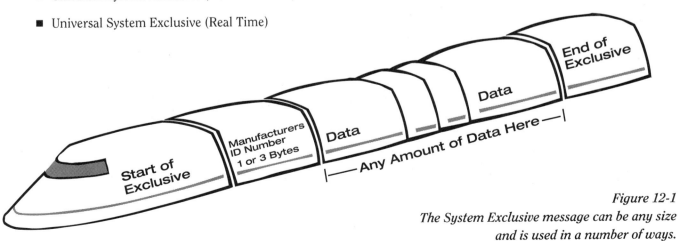

Figure 12-1
The System Exclusive message can be any size
and is used in a number of ways.

System Exclusive messages are used in a number of ways:

- Sending patch parameter information from a MIDI instrument to a computer for storage or editing.

- Transmitting the patterns from one drum machine to another, or to a computer.

- Transmitting the memory of a digital sampler to a computer for editing or to another sampler.

- Sending song data from a stand-alone sequencer to another sequencer or a computer for storage.

- Manipulating individual parameters from the front panel of an instrument for use as a remote control by another of the same instrument.

Figure 12-1 shows the format of a System Exclusive message. The first byte is the Status message for System Exclusive. The second byte is the *Manufacturer's Identification* number. Every manufacturer of MIDI instruments is given a unique ID number for all of their products by one of two official MIDI standards organizations. For all Japanese manufacturers the organization is the Japanese MIDI Standards Committee (JMSC). The rest of the world is governed by the MIDI Manufacturers Association (MMA). A manufacturer uses the same ID number for all their products that need System Exclusive. Each company has complete control over the format and content of any System Exclusive messages using their ID number. These formats are not secrets, and can usually be found in the back of most instrument's manual. Other companies can make products compatible with those Sysex codes, if they wish, but they may not change anything about it. For example, there are MIDI data storage devices that use manufacturers' Sysex codes to command an instrument to transmit its entire memory via Sysex and store it on a floppy disk for later recall.

System Exclusive messages don't have a normal MIDI Channel number. When an instrument receives a "Start of Exclusive" byte, it first checks the following Manufacturer ID number to see if it matches its own brand or not. If the ID number is from a different company, the receiver ignores the rest of the data until the "End Of Exclusive" byte is received to indicate the packet is finished.

The code immediately after the manufacturer ID is the instrument's model number. Once again, the receiver determines if the message is specifically for it, or possibly for another type of instrument made by the same company. If the model identification is different, it will ignore the rest of the message.

Usually, there is information immediately following the ID number to indicate the type of instrument and the MIDI channel of the sender. After that, the actual data is sent. A System Exclusive message always concludes with the "End Of Exclusive" message.

There is no predetermined number of data bytes within a System Exclusive message. There will be as many bytes as are needed to send the information along. A typical single patch may be anywhere from a few dozen to several hundred bytes of data. MIDI instruments have a *bulk dump* function that will send the entire contents of their memories. A bulk dump can be thousands of bytes long.

Programmable synthesizers all use memory cards for storing banks of patches. Those cards can be used to move a bank of patches from one to another of the same instrument. So why the need for Sysex? One of the most functional uses is for the transfer of the memory contents of instruments to a computer for storage, organization, and later retrieval. Using your computer and an *editor/librarian* software program to keep track of large volumes of patches makes it possible to find any "needle in the haystack" patch quickly. (See more on these software programs in *Chapter 13*.)

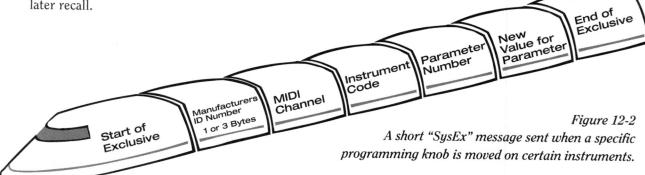

Figure 12-2
A short "SysEx" message sent when a specific programming knob is moved on certain instruments.

System Exclusive messages are also used by some instruments to transmit information about individual buttons, sliders, or knobs that are in use on its front panel. As a button is pushed or a knob turned, a short Sysex message is sent that indicates which knob is being manipulated and its current position. **Figure 12-2** is an example.

Sysex messages are used, since information about a knob on a synthesizer is not of use to anything other than that model of synthesizer.

By sending information over MIDI that indicates how the front panel of a synthesizer is being manipulated, it is possible to use one instrument as a programming remote control for another. This is useful for creating or modifying patches in a rack-mounted MIDI sound module that may not have front panel knobs. These codes are used by computer-based patch editors for manipulating a single parameter of a synthesizer. They can also be recorded into most sequencers as part of a composition. Upon playback, the same parameters will change, allowing for interesting changes in the sound as the music plays.

While the primary focus of Sysex codes is for information about specific synthesizers, the role of Sysex has expanded over the years to include some of MIDI's most powerful features. These fall under the second two categories mentioned above—Universal

Figure 12-3: Rack-mount synthesizers can be programmed via MIDI System Exclusive

System Exclusive (Non-Real Time), and Universal System Exclusive (Real Time). These are codes used in more sophisticated MIDI systems that describe information that is *not related to the playing of musical notes*. You've already learned about one such System Exclusive code—MIDI Time Code—discussed in *Chapter 10*. **Figure 12-4** is a listing of all currently defined System Exclusive message types.

Universal System Exclusive messages are distinguished by the use of reserved Manufacturer ID numbers, the second byte of the Sysex message. One is used for all real time messages, those sent during a musical performance to trigger non-musical events, and the other for non-real time messages, those sent outside of a musical performance, which don't trigger events. On the following page is a description of Universal Sysex's more important features (see Chapter 10 for a description of MIDI Time Code):

Non-Real Time (7EH)		Real Time (7FH)	
SUB-ID #1	**DESCRIPTION**	**SUB-ID #1**	**DESCRIPTION**
00	Unused	00	Unused
01	Sample Dump Header	01	MIDI Time Code
02	Sample Data Packet	02	MIDI Show Control
03	Sample Dump Request	03	Notation Information
04	MIDI Time Code	04	Device Control
05	Sample Dump Extensions	05	Real Time MTC Cueing
06	General Information	06	MIDI Machine Control Commands
07	File Dump	07	MIDI Machine Control Responses
08	MIDI Tuning Standard	08	MIDI Tuning Standard
09	General MIDI		
7B	End Of File		
7C	Wait		
7D	Cancel		
7E	NAK		
7F	ACK		

Figure 12-4 Universal System Exclusive types.

■ Sample Dump Standard

A *sampler* is a musical instrument that produces a sound by digitally recording an acoustic sound and then playing it back from a keyboard or in response to MIDI messages. Samplers have memories far larger than most synthesizers, into the tens of megabytes (millions of bytes).

Computer programs to edit and manipulate samples are available for several brands of computers and most samplers. A copy of the sampler's memory is sent out in a very long System Exclusive message to the computer. The computer program visually displays the *waveforms* of the sampled sound on its screen, and allows them to be manipulated. The samples can be returned to the sampler, saved to the computer's disk, or converted and sent to another model of sampler.

At first, the format in which samples were transmitted via MIDI was different for each instrument. There was no standard. Then, in 1986, a standard for *sample dumps* was adopted for all MIDI samplers. The *Sample Dump Standard*, as it is called, is a non-real time Universal System Exclusive format for sending and receiving samples through MIDI for all samplers. Now, samples can be sent from one sampler to another, or from a sampler to a computer.

All samplers that support the Sample Dump Standard have a *Get Sample* and *Send Sample* function. Selecting a sample and Send Sample causes the sampler to send the *dump header* message. This message contains information about the sample, such as its size and name, and other technical details. If another sampler is connected to the sender, on the same MIDI channel, and is ready to receive a sample, it will send an acknowledgment that it is ready to receive the sample. This is called a *handshake*. These handshakes are sent between the two machines every few dozen bytes to ensure that none of the data gets lost or mixed up. The use of handshakes means that in order to use sample dumping, you need two MIDI cables, OUT to IN, and IN to OUT.

A sampler or computer program can also ask for a sample to be sent via MIDI with a Sysex message called a *Dump Request*. This message, which also has a handshake, asks for a particular sample in the sampler's memory to be sent right away. Upon receiving the message, the sampler begins sending the sample just as described above. Because of their size, samples dumped with MIDI Sysex can take anywhere from a few seconds to several minutes to transfer from sampler to computer or vice versa.

■ General Information

One of MIDI's weaknesses is the inability of a computer to know what devices are in the system. Other intelligent computer networks can detect the presence of specific devices and address their particular needs. Not in MIDI. This issue is taken up in the form of *Identity Request* and *Identity Reply* messages, both under the heading of *General Information*. When an instrument receives the Identity Request message, it sends information about itself in the form of an Identity Reply message. The information can include the make and model of the instrument, the number of channels to which it can respond, its polyphony, the current patch names in its memory, and so forth. This can only be found on a very limited number of instruments, and only ones made after 1990, when General Information was added to the MIDI specification.

■ File Dump

This message works much like the sample dump message, but instead of sending samples from instrument to instrument, it sends other types of data, including *Standard MIDI Files,* (see *Chapter 13* for information) from sequencer to sequencer, or from computer to computer. Data such as Standard MIDI Files can be exchanged by disk, but if the disk formats between the two machines are not compatible, then there needs to be another way to get the song file from one machine to the other. File Dump can send a sequence in far less time than the sequence takes to actually play.

■ General MIDI On/Off

General MIDI, described in great detail in *Chapter 14*, is a special mode built into some synthesizers. This Sysex message commands a General MIDI-compatible instrument to either enter or leave its General MIDI mode.

■ MIDI Show Control

MIDI has become of great use in many non-musical applications. One interesting example is MIDI Show Control (MSC). MSC is a group of Universal Sysex Real Time messages for automating theatrical performances by specifying the exact moment to change lighting, open or close curtains, fire off pyrotechnics, operate a hydraulic lift and other stage devices, and coordinate the action with musical cues from sequencers, tape or other types of recordings. MSC-compatible theaters can be controlled by a simple MIDI program running on a computer with compatible lighting consoles and other control equipment.

■ Notation Information

This set of Real Time messages allows a sequencer or other MIDI performance program to send out the current time signature and bar number of the music playing. The message can be received and displayed on a screen by another program. This function is primarily for use by specialized non-sequencing software, for education uses or for less commercial applications.

■ Device Control

MIDI Continuous Controller #7 adjusts the volume of a synthesizer. Multitimbral instruments have many channels, so a separate MIDI Volume message controls each channel. *Device Control* is made up of two messages, *Master Volume* and *Master Balance*. The master volume message sets the overall volume of an entire multitimbral instrument, not just a single channel. Likewise, the left/right balance of the entire instrument can be set with the Master Balance message. These messages retain the relative volumes of each channel as set by Controller #7 and #8.

■ MIDI Machine Control

The ability to slave a sequencer to tape opens up a great number of musical possibilities (see *Chapter 17*). But what if you could control an audio tape machine or video deck from your MIDI sequencer? You would have a far more musical system. Standard tape machines can be located to a given spot in a song by specifying the position in time (minutes and seconds) or by a meaningless counter ("go to 1:34 on the tape and play"). A sequencer thinks in musical terms, like bars and beats, verses and choruses. MIDI Machine Control (MMC) gives control over a wide range of audio and video equipment from a sequencer or other MIDI program. It is tremendously powerful. Through MMC, a sequencer can command a tape machine to locate to a point in a song, begin playing, stay synchronized to the sequencer, and even punch in and out of *record* on any desired track ("Go to bar 29 and record on Track 6").

MIDI messages travel in both directions between a computer-based sequencer and the tape machine. **Figure 12-5** is a diagram of how an MMC system is setup:

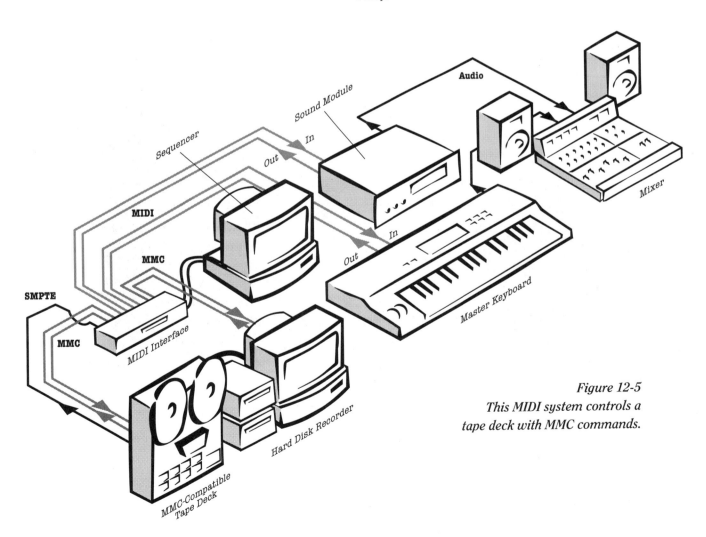

Figure 12-5
This MIDI system controls a tape deck with MMC commands.

■ MIDI Tuning Standard

Since the time of Johann Sebastian Bach, the bulk of all western music is based on an "even tempered" 12-tone scale. All instruments, acoustic and electronic, are tuned this way and western musicians are taught to play exclusively in this scale. Yet, there are other scales and instrument tunings from other cultures around the world, or from before Bach's time, which are rarely used or heard anymore. These scales have a sound quite different than most people are used to—some very sonorous and some highly dissonant. The interest in some of the "alternative" tunings has continued to grow in recent years.* Synthesizer tunings and scales can be anything desired, since everything about them must be specifically designed and programmed. Many synthesizers now come with many alternative scales, and are even user-programmable. What was needed was a way to reprogram the tuning of a synthesizer from within a sequencer or special tuning program. Thus was born the *MIDI Tuning Standard*, which consists of one Non-Real Time and one Real Time message.

The non-real time message can either send an entire scale to an instrument, or get a scale from an instrument, similar to sample or file dump.

However, some scales require that one or two notes be retuned as the key of the music changes. For this there is the Real Time *Note Change* message, which allows a single note of the scale to be redefined.

USING SYSTEM EXCLUSIVE

The need for using System Exclusive will come up only when you wish to send program data from one instrument to another, to a computer for storage or manipulation, or for some available non-musical applications for MIDI. The techniques for doing this are different for each MIDI instrument and program, so you must consult the manuals.

If you are working with a sequencer that is able to record System Exclusive messages along with other MIDI data, you may wish to enable the instrument to send System Exclusive, if possible. By doing this, any program changes made while recording the piece will record not only the program number, but all the parameter data of the patch itself. By implementing this, you no longer need to remember what patches were loaded in the synthesizer when the music was recorded. As the sequence plays back, the original sounds used during the recording will be sent to the instrument and played.

Always turn down the volume before turning on any amplifier!

To learn more about alternative tunings, see "Tuning In: Microtonality in Electronic Music" *by Scott Wilkinson, published by Hal Leonard Publications.*

13

MIDI and the Personal Computer

When MIDI first appeared, musicians saw it and said "It is good!" (actually, it was more like "Hey man, this is like, cool!"). But the real power and glory only occurred when MIDI met the personal computer (PC). With the right software and MIDI interface, a PC becomes one of the most useful "instruments" in your MIDI system.

If you don't have a computer, how do you choose the one for you? There are four factors involved in your decision: software, price, what your friends use, and software (okay, there are only three factors).

As of this writing, the computers most often found in the MIDI studio are the Apple Macintosh, the IBM PC (and all compatibles), Atari computers, and, to a much lesser extent, the Commodore Amiga. When considering a computer, you need to look at the available software options to decide on the computer that performs best for you (and your bank account). If you intend to collaborate with someone already using a computer, then you might want to have the same system, unless they seem unhappy with their choice of machine.

Many of the functions for which musicians use computers can be done without one. After all, a lot of great music gets made without a computer. The same is true, to a lesser extent for the MIDI musician. It is possible to build a studio without a computer, relying on stand-alone sequencers and patch storage devices in addition to your synthesizers and other instruments. But you would be missing out on a lot.

The computer's versatility has made it become nearly indispensable in the MIDI studio. It can do just about anything. There are other advantages, which you won't get with stand-alone MIDI equipment, such as:

- Large, colorful display

- Ability to perform many helpful non-music functions

- Ability to store massive amounts of musical information

- An excellent selection of musical and non-musical software

- Can perform new tasks with a simple software purchase

- Can improve its abilities with (often free) software upgrades

A computer can perform a great many tasks in a MIDI studio. With the right hardware and software, it becomes the central brain around which everything revolves (including you). Here is a list with some of the most useful duties you can perform with a PC:

- Compose music

- Print your music on paper

- Keep a sequenced musical sketchbook

- Keep a lyric sketchbook

- Store your library of synthesizer patches on disk

- Program new synthesizer sounds graphically

- Edit samples

- Practice ear training

- Find words that rhyme

- Learn about music theory and history

- Study Beethoven

- Send MIDI Files to a friend by modem

- Edit your next video

In order for a computer to do anything, the proper software is needed. The software for musical applications is usually found in music stores rather than in computer stores.

Here are the main types of software programs for the MIDI musician:

■ Sequencers

This is the most essential piece of software you should get for your studio. A MIDI sequencer allows you to record your performance into the computer. Once there, it can be fixed, edited, modified, and molded any way you wish. A sequencer operates similarly to a multitrack audio recorder. Music goes onto namable tracks, which are assigned to one or more MIDI channels upon playback.

Most sequencers also provide the ability to compose a song in segments and then assemble the segments in any order into a song. Segments can be used over and over without the need to re-perform any of the material.

After the music has been recorded, a sequencer can display it in a number of ways in order to change any notes or other MIDI events. The editing capabilities of MIDI sequencing are vast. For the less technically accomplished musician, music can be performed very slowly into the sequencer, and played back at normal speed without the accompanying change in pitch one would get from audio tape.

Sequencers also offer rhythmic *quantization*, which corrects small rhythmic errors in a performance without manual editing. Plus, most computer sequencers provide a transcription of your performance into standard music notation, or can export a special file to another program capable of reading the file and then making the transcription (see the section on *Standard MIDI Files* later in this chapter).

■ Patch Librarians

As you create or collect more patches for your instruments, you will no longer be able to store all of them in the instrument. You will need to keep them elsewhere. You can use *RAM cards*, which store banks of sounds for any given instrument. These are expensive and difficult to organize. The best way to

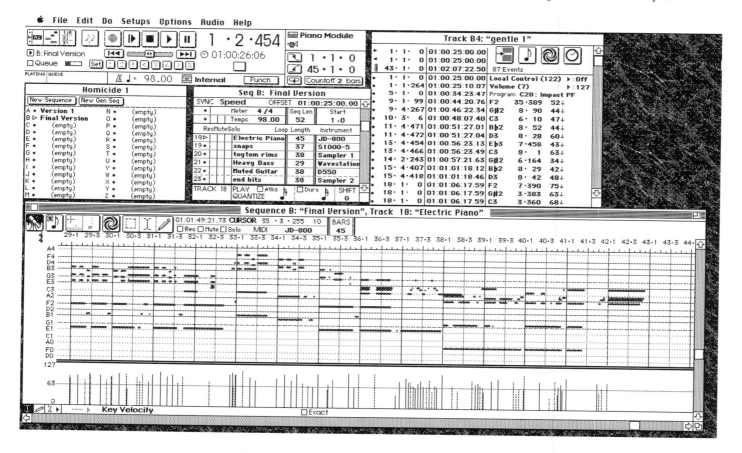

Figure 13-1 A computer-based MIDI sequencer.

manage large groups of sounds is with a computer program called a *patch librarian* (**Figure 13-2**). As the name implies, a librarian helps to organize and find a patch or group of patches for which you are looking. A librarian program, which is designed to work with a specific MIDI instrument, will cause all the parameter data from the memory of the synthesizer to be sent to the computer via MIDI Sysex. Once in the computer, the patch names are displayed on the screen. You can now reorganize the sounds in any way you wish: alphabetical, by category or type of sound, and so forth. You can also combine sounds from one bank with others you have in the computer. However, you can not change the patches themselves. Once you have everything the way you wish, the new banks can be saved to disk, and a new bank can be sent and stored in the synthesizer by Sysex.

A patch librarian needs to know specific information about a synthesizer in order to send, receive and

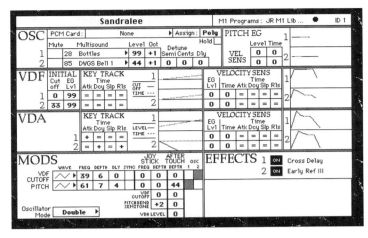

Figure 13-3 A Patch Editor presents a synthesizer's parameters in a graphic manner.

vide a larger and more complete picture of a synthesizer's patch parameters. If you are seriously interested in creating your own sounds and have a programmable synthesizer, a patch editor (**Figure 13-3**) will save you time and trouble.

■ Sample Editors

What a patch editor does for a synthesizer, a sample editor does for samplers and digitally-sampled sounds. The actual digital waveforms can be transferred from a sampler to the computer for better display (see **Figure 13-4**) and manipulation, and then returned to the sampler for playback and storage. The Sysex Sample

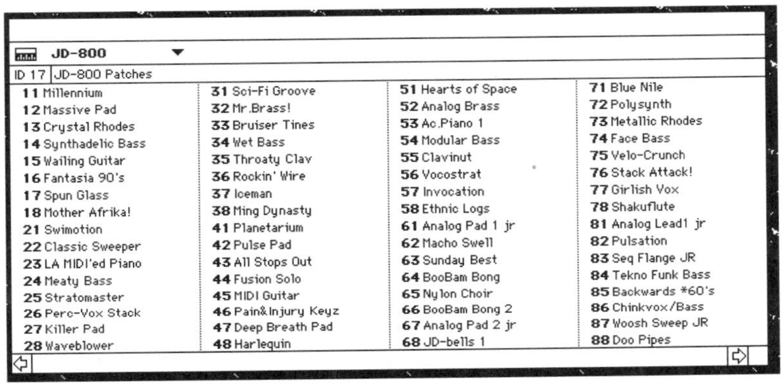

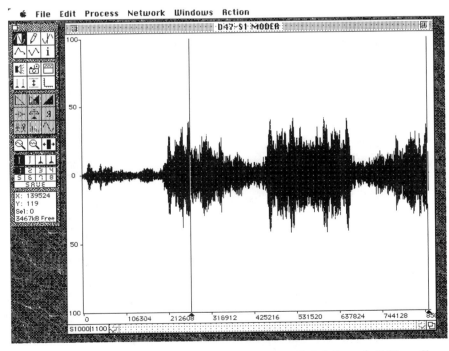

Figure 13-2 A Patch Librarian allows easy organization of a synthesizer's memory.

handle the data from the instrument's memory. Thus, a librarian must be created for each supported instrument. There are, however, *universal librarians*, which are a single program able to support most or all of the instruments in your studio. These can be upgraded to support newer synthesizers as they become available.

■ Patch Editor/Librarians

There are more sophisticated programs that, in addition to the chores of a patch librarian, allow you to actually manipulate and modify the synthesizer's patches right from the screen of your computer. The advantage of this is the computer can pro-

Figure 13-4 A Sample Editor allows manipulation of sample waveforms.

Dump Standard is used to request and transfer waveform data between the computer and the sampler.

■ Notation

From the moment that MIDI sequencers became available for the personal computer, musicians have wanted a program that would take a performance and transcribe it into standard music notation. Eventually those programs became available, either as a part of a sequencer or a separate program. Though the technology of music transcription isn't perfect, there are many programs that do an excellent job of creating musical scores and parts from a MIDI performance. Separate music notation programs can read Standard MIDI Files (see below) in order to transcribe a part from a MIDI sequencer.

Figure 13-5 A computer can transcribe a MIDI sequence into standard music notation.

■ Educational

While not a replacement for a good teacher, there are computer programs that can teach music theory, test skills and help with ear training. Some programs work with MIDI, while others use the simple built-in sound capabilities of the computer.

■ Interactive Software

For the more musically adventurous, come programs to create music by means other than simply recording a performance from a MIDI instrument. Interactive programs allow you to create

"intelligent" musical "toys" on the screen of the computer. These MIDI toys can actually improvise and play a piece of music based on rules you specify. embellish an incoming MIDI performance with additional musical parts or almost anything you can dream up. The catch is that you have to put some

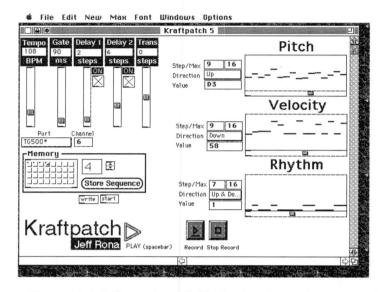

Figure 13-6 Software is available for the advanced MIDI user to create unique custom applications.

time into creating the "toy" yourself. Some systems are more complex than others with which to create your own unique applications. Not for the digitally squeamish.

■ Digital Audio Workstations

With some additional audio hardware, a large capacity hard drive and some software, your computer can become a state-of-the-art digital audio recording and editing system. These systems are capable of editing sound, either in stereo or multitrack formats. You can rearrange, shorten or elongate a song after it has

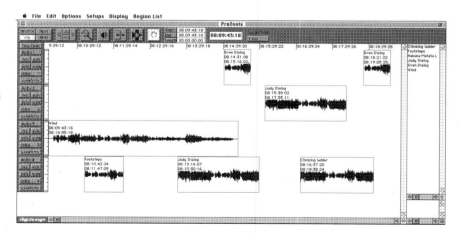

Figure 13-7 The computer can be used for sophisticated tapeless audio recording and editing.

been recorded and mixed, edit together a demo or final album from several recordings, or synchronize audio with video. Similar programs are available that allow you to edit the video as well, so now you can make your own videos right on your computer. However, video systems are very expensive.

WHAT ELSE?

So there it is, a beautiful new computer sitting in the middle of your studio. You've just written your best song with it and now you want to take a day or two off from music. What else is a computer good for? The answer, in a word, is *lots*. Here is a list of just a few productive things you can do outside of MIDI with a personal computer:

- Write a letter
- Make an invoice
- Balance your checkbook
- Check the spelling of everything you write
- Schedule your tour
- Remember appointments
- Write a book
- Budget your next album
- Send faxes
- Design a cover for your demo or album
- Label and organize your tapes
- Send messages anywhere in the world
- Receive electronic mail from anywhere in the world
- Get free software by modem
- Play chess
- Learn about any topic in the world

YOU MEAN THERE'S MORE?

Buying a computer is a lot like getting married, you suddenly have a whole new family to get to know. Getting the most from a computer often means adding on certain options, called *peripherals*. To expand your system, here are some of the items you may want:

■ MIDI Interface

Mandatory, of course! (Only Atari has built MIDI

right in to their computers.) Interfaces for other computers are available with different options. Some provide extensive synchronization-to-tape capabilities, some provide extra MIDI ports, which allow you to address more than 16 MIDI channels in your studio. Most larger interfaces also function as MIDI *patchbays*, to help route MIDI data in and out of the instruments in your studio.

■ Larger monitor or more colors

Many computer's are designed so that using a bigger *monitor* (the computer's video display screen) lets you see more information at a time, instead of making the picture larger. If you create sequences with a lot of tracks, this is very handy. Color, while not a necessity for music, makes looking at your screen for hours every day far more enjoyable. Many graphics programs require color.

■ Printer

If you want to print musical scores, parts, or anything else, you need a printer compatible with your computer. They are available in different qualities, usually expressed in DPI, or Dot Per Inch. More is better.

■ Modem

A modem allows you to share files from your computer with other computer users. There are also many *on-line services*, which provide free software, games, and other information to people with modems. Some are geared exclusively to electronic musicians (see the offer for PAN in *"For More Information"*). A modem connects your computer to others through ordinary telephone lines. Better modems are faster and add the capability of sending and receiving faxes right from your computer.

■ Extra memory

When you purchase a computer, it comes with some nominal amount of RAM, which is the memory you need to hold information as you work with it. You can purchase additional RAM in the form of chips made specifically for your model of computer. More memory allows you to make sequences with more notes, hold more patches or bigger samples at one time, or run many programs simultaneously.

■ Hard Drive

The memory in your computer only stores information as long as the power is on. Once you shut it off, the RAM memory in the computer will lose everything. Not a pleasant idea. Computers all come equipped with a floppy disk drive and at least the capacity to add a hard drive (though most come with a hard drive already inside). A hard drive is able to store and recall information far faster than floppy disks, and the capacity of hard drives exceeds floppies by many times, making them a valuable form of data storage. Floppies are best used for taking a file from your computer to another, and for making safety copies of the files on your hard drive. Most hard drives for PCs use a standard interface called *SCSI*, which stands for Small Computer Systems Interface. It's like MIDI for hard drives.

Some hard drives use *removable media*. Once they are filled up, a special cartridge, which holds all the information, can be popped out of the drive and replaced with a new cartridge.

■ A Bigger Hard Drive

As you begin to collect more and more software and files, you may begin to run out of space on your hard drive. Fortunately, you can get hard drives with extraordinary capacity. These are required if you are considering doing any digital audio recording or sample storage.

■ CD ROM Drive

Most of the software you purchase for your computer will come on one or more floppy disks. But there are programs that are so massive, they could barely fit on a large-capacity hard drive. Programs that offer hours of graphics or sound, an entire encyclopedia with moving pictures, games with gigantic amounts of pictures and sound, entire movies viewable on your computer, dozens of color photographs, or databases of tremendous size and scope are available, but in a different form.

These kinds of programs are available on a type of disk called CD–ROM, which stands for *Compact Disc–Read Only Memory*. They look exactly like standard audio CDs, and in fact use much of the same technology. However, instead of storing digital audio, they store all types of digital information—sound, pictures, and software programs. In order to use a CD-ROM with your computer, you need a CD-ROM drive that plugs into the SCSI port on your PC. You *can not* save your own files onto CD-ROM. Some CD-ROM drives will play audio CDs right on your computer, or you can get a boom-box for your computer, and plug it in.

■ Scanner

If you are interested in making graphics with your PC, a scanner can be very handy. It operates like a photocopier, but instead of copying a picture onto paper, anything put into a scanner will be digitized and put inside the computer. Once there, and with the right software, you can manipulate photos or drawings and integrate them together with other text or graphics for professional looking artwork. There is software available that can scan sheet music and convert it into a Standard MIDI File.

STANDARD MIDI FILES

In a perfect world, there would exist a MIDI sequencer that would do it all: run on your choice of computer, have every feature you could ever want, transcribe your music into standard notation, offer unusual music improvising algorithms, run on every computer, and be a snap to learn and use. Until that day comes (*author's note: don't hold your breath*), there is a way to exchange MIDI sequences between various programs and computers called a *Standard MIDI File*, MIDI File for short, and SMF for very short. The MIDI File is a different part of MIDI called a *Recommended Practice*, which are official "suggestions" by MIDI's developers for ways to help other parts of a MIDI system to work better. None are mandatory, but they help to create more compatibility between different instruments or programs. Recommended Practices are not like the typical MIDI messages, and aren't transmitted over MIDI cables.

MIDI Files are a standard computer file format agreed to by all the manufacturers of computer-based sequencers, and sanctioned as a Recommended Practice. With MIDI Files, sequences created and saved to disk with one MIDI program can be loaded into any other MIDI File-compatible program (called *importing*), or be moved from one computer to another.

Most MIDI sequencers offer two options for saving music to disk. Sequences saved normally can only be opened and read by the program that created them. The other option is to save the music as a Standard MIDI File. Now, the file can be opened and used by all other MIDI File compatible programs. All information about a sequence is stored in a MIDI File, including notes, controllers, patch changes, tempo, tempo changes (called the tempo map), meter changes, and track names.

There are three types of MIDI files, each for a particular use:

- *Type 0* **stores the music as a single, multi-channel track.** This format is for music that need never be edited again. It is used by programs that do simple playback of sequences. This format is also used for exchanging only tempo and meter information from one program to another.

- *Type 1* **keeps all the original tracks separated.** This format is used by most sequencers and music notation programs for exchanging sequences. It is the format used by any sequencer that does not use musical segments in order to build a song from parts.

- *Type 2* **keeps all original tracks and separate multiple sequences**. This format keeps everything intact and separate. A sequence that uses multiple segments will remain as segments.

TIPS FOR COMPUTER OWNERS

Here are some brief thoughts to keep in mind if you are using a computer in your studio.

- **Don't turn it on and off many times each day** – it will last longer if it is turned on no more than once or twice a day. If you are only leaving for a few hours, simply leave it running.

- **Use a screen saver to preserve the monitor longer** – a screen saver is an inexpensive software utility that puts random moving pictures on your computer screen after a few minutes of inactivity. It prevents the image from burning into the screen if you happen to leave it on for very long periods of time.

- **Back up the hard drive often** – hard drives all crash eventually, and when your time comes you stand a chance at losing everything on it. Get into the habit of regularly copying all the data from your hard drive to a set of floppies, or another hard drive. There are a number of programs that help automate the process.

- **Keep it cool and dust free** – Heat and dust can shorten the life of a computer, its drive and many of the peripherals.

- **Place the cables so they can not be tripped over** – accidents do happen. Be sure they don't happen to you.

- **Always power on any external disk drives before the computer** – In order for your computer to properly detect the presence of any external hard drives, they must be powered-on first.

- **Save your work often** – As you are composing, editing or anything else, it is easy not to think about the fact that if the power goes out, you will lose all your work. Most programs will save your work–in–progress with a single button. The hard part is remembering to do it. Get into the habit of saving your work every time you do something you like.

- **If it crashes, don't panic** – Computers do and will crash, usually at the least opportune moment. When a computer seems to freeze up, don't worry. No real damage has occurred, though you'll probably lose whatever you were working on at the time.

- **Learn the computer's operating system well** – The operating system is the software that permits the computer to power up, run other software, use a disk drive, make copies of files, and all the other routine chores that the computer does to earn its keep. Every computer has one, and each comes with a manual. Knowing how your computer works will save you time and effort in the long run.

- **Don't steal software** – Computer software comes on floppy disks, which are easily copied right on the computer. It's so easy to do that people forget that it's illegal. It is the same as photocopying a friend's book or taping a friend's CD. Buying software instead of copying it pays for the programmers to keep making better and better programs for you to use. Much of MIDI software is copy protected, which prevents illegal copying, though it makes the software more difficult to install, and you must get a new copy if the hard disk crashes.

MIDI Files make moving a sequence from one program to another on the same computer as automatic as saving and loading a file. Moving a MIDI File from one computer to another is a bit more complicated. While a MIDI File is the same for any computer, not all computers can accept and read disks made by another brand of computer. This problem can be overcome either by sending the file by modem, or by using a special program that lets a computer read disks from other machines.

MIDI Files have helped to integrate music software applications by allowing them to freely exchange files. If one program offers a special editing feature not found on another that you enjoy using, simply save the music as a MIDI File, run the other program and open that same file. Virtually all MIDI and music-related software support the use of Standard MIDI Files.

Personal computers are powerful and easy to use!

14

General MIDI

Not everyone becomes involved with MIDI and electronic instruments because they want to create all kinds of new sounds. Some of us are just musicians who want a palette of good sounds with which to compose and perform. A need arose in the computer world for better sound in games and multimedia. Those needs were recognized, and a new part of the MIDI standard was born. Welcome to General MIDI.

Figure 14-1 This logo is found on all General MIDI instruments.

No, not a high ranking musical military officer, General MIDI (GM) is an unusual part of the MIDI specification called a *recommended practice*. It isn't a MIDI message or command. Instead, it is a description of a class of musical instruments that all share a consistent set of features and capabilities. This means that music created for playback on a GM instrument will sound musically consistent on *any* GM instrument.

A typical MIDI system is very personalized. You choose the instruments you want to use and the sounds that are in each instrument. Manufacturers developing new synthesizers are free to put any kind of sounds in the machine they wish, in any order. Sequences you record in your studio with your equipment will not automatically fit into other MIDI systems. You will need to put some amount of effort

in to redirecting channels and changing patch change messages to fit the new gear you are using.

All of this extra noodling disappears with GM. Any instrument that bears the mighty GM logo must adhere to a predetermined list of features and patch assignments. What are the exact specifications of a GM synth? They include:

■ 24 voices of polyphony in order to play back very full arrangements

■ Respond to all 16 MIDI channels

■ Each channel can access any number of voices (*dynamic voice allocation*)

■ Each channel can play a different timbre (multitimbral)

■ A full set of percussion instruments is available on Channel 10

■ All percussion instruments are mapped to specific MIDI note numbers

■ A minimum of 128 presets available as MIDI Program numbers

■ All sounds are available on all MIDI channels (except 10, which is for percussion)

■ All GM instruments and percussion respond to Note On velocity

■ Middle C is always note number 60

■ All GM instruments can respond to these MIDI Controllers:

1	Modulation
7	Volume
10	Pan
11	Expression
64	Sustain Pedal
121	Reset All Controllers
123	All Notes Off

- GM instruments respond to all Registered Parameters

0	Pitch Bend Sensitivity
1	Fine Tuning
2	Coarse Tuning

- GM instruments all respond to these additional MIDI messages:

Channel Pressure (Aftertouch)
Pitch Bend (with a default of two semitones)

Perhaps most importantly, GM doesn't leave the order of the patches in a synthesizers memory to chance. At the heart of the GM system is the *GM Sound Set*. It specifies the exact sound, by name, for each of the 128 sounds in the synthesizer. For example, Patch #1 must always be an acoustic grand piano on all channels (except 10 which is reserved for drums and percussion) on all GM instruments. All other patch locations are also organized to conform to the GM Sound Set.

Anyone who creates a sequence for playback using a GM synthesizer, called a *General MIDI Score*, need only to look at the Sound Set map, and send the appropriate patch changes to call up the desired sound. Drum and percussion parts are similar, since the same MIDI note numbers will always trigger the same sound. Channel 10 is reserved exclusively for drums and percussion. All other channels are available for the other parts of your arrangement.

Piano		Bass		Reed		Synth Effects	
1.	Acoustic Grand Piano	33.	Acoustic Bass	65.	Soprano Sax	97.	FX 1 (rain)
2.	Bright Acoustic Piano	34.	Electric Bass (finger)	66.	Alto Sax	98.	FX 2 (soundtrack)
3.	Electric Grand Piano	35.	Electric Bass (pick)	67.	Tenor Sax	99.	FX 3 (crystal)
4.	Honky-tonk Piano	36.	Fretless Bass	68.	Baritone Sax	100.	FX 4 (atmosphere)
5.	Electric Piano 1	37.	Slap Bass 1	69.	Oboe	101.	FX 5 (brightness)
6.	Electric Piano 2	38.	Slap Bass 2	70.	English Horn	102.	FX 6 (goblins)
7.	Harpsichord	39.	Synth Bass 1	71.	Bassoon	103.	FX 7 (echoes)
8.	Clavi	40.	Synth Bass 2	72.	Clarinet	104.	FX 8 (sci-fi)
Chromatic Percussion		**Strings**		**Pipe**		**Ethnic**	
9.	Celesta	41.	Violin	73.	Piccolo	105.	Sitar
10.	Glockenspiel	42.	Viola	74.	Flute	106.	Banjo
11.	Music Box	43.	Cello	75.	Recorder	107.	Shamisen
12.	Vibraphone	44.	Contrabass	76.	Pan Flute	108.	Koto
13.	Marimba	45.	Tremolo Strings	77.	Blown Bottle	109.	Kalimba
14.	Xylophone	46.	Pizzicato Strings	78.	Shakuhachi	110.	Bag pipe
15.	Tubular Bells	47.	Orchestral Harp	79.	Whistle	111.	Fiddle
16.	Dulcimer	48.	Timpani	80.	Ocarina	112.	Shanai
Organ		**Ensemble**		**Synth Lead**		**Percussive**	
17.	Drawbar Organ	49.	String Ensemble 1	81.	Lead 1 (square)	113.	Tinkle Bell
18.	Percussive Organ	50.	String Ensemble 2	82.	Lead 2 (sawtooth)	114.	Agogo
19.	Rock Organ	51.	SynthStrings 1	83.	Lead 3 (calliope)	115.	Steel Drums
20.	Church Organ	52.	SynthStrings 2	84.	Lead 4 (chiff)	116.	Woodblock
21.	Reed Organ	53.	Choir Aahs	85.	Lead 5 (charang)	117.	Taiko Drum
22.	Accordion	54.	Voice Oohs	86.	Lead 6 (voice)	118.	Melodic Tom
23.	Harmonica	55.	Synth Voice	87.	Lead 7 (fifths)	119.	Synth Drum
24.	Tango Accordion	56.	Orchestra Hit	88.	Lead 8 (bass + lead)	120.	Reverse Cymbal
Guitar		**Brass**		**Synth Pad**		**Sound Effects**	
25.	Acoustic Guitar (nylon)	57.	Trumpet	89.	Pad 1 (new age)	121.	Guitar Fret Noise
26.	Acoustic Guitar (steel)	58.	Trombone	90.	Pad 2 (warm)	122.	Breath Noise
27.	Electric Guitar (jazz)	59.	Tuba	91.	Pad 3 (polysynth)	123.	Seashore
28.	Electric Guitar (clean)	60.	Muted Trumpet	92.	Pad 4 (choir)	124.	Bird Tweet
29.	Electric Guitar (muted)	61.	French Horn	93.	Pad 5 (bowed)	125.	Telephone Ring
30.	Overdriven Guitar	62.	Brass Section	94.	Pad 6 (metallic)	126.	Helicopter
31.	Distortion Guitar	63.	SynthBrass 1	95.	Pad 7 (halo)	127.	Applause
32.	Guitar harmonics	64.	SynthBrass 2	96.	Pad 8 (sweep)	128.	Gunshot

Figure 14-2 The GM sound set.

35.	Acoustic Bass Drum	51.	Ride Cymbal 1	67.	High Agogo
36.	Bass Drum 1	52.	Chinese Cymbal	68.	Low Agogo
37.	Side Stick	53.	Ride Bell	69.	Cabasa
38.	Acoustic Snare	54.	Tambourine	70.	Maracas
39.	Hand Clap	55.	Splash Cymbal	71.	Short Whistle
40.	Electric Snare	56.	Cowbell	72.	Long Whistle
41.	Low Floor Tom	57.	Crash Cymbal 2	73.	Short Guiro
42.	Closed Hi Hat	58.	Vibraslap	74.	Long Guiro
43.	High Floor Tom	59.	Ride Cymbal 2	75.	Claves
44.	Pedal Hi-Hat	60.	Hi Bongo	76.	Hi Wood Block
45.	Low Tom	61.	Low Bongo	77.	Low Wood Block
46.	Open Hi-Hat	62.	Mute Hi Conga	78.	Mute Cuica
47.	Low-Mid Tom	63.	Open Hi Conga	79.	Open Cuica
48.	Hi Mid Tom	64.	Low Conga	80.	Mute Triangle
49.	Crash Cymbal 1	65.	High Timbale	81.	Open Triangle
50.	High Tom	66.	Low Timbale		

Figure 14-3 the GM Percussion Set.

With all these specifications in common, there is a great deal of compatibility among all GM instruments. What differentiates them is *how* they sound. GM doesn't dictate the technology that a manufacturer should use to create their sounds. Some instruments have far better sound quality than others, but all are capable of playing the same music with nearly exact results musically.

THE PURPOSE OF GM

General MIDI was not designed for the professional or semiprofessional composer/musician interested in putting together a MIDI system for their own work. The restrictions of GM outweigh the features, though there are some very good sounding GM synthesizers available. Some synthesizers on the market are both GM compatible or not, depending on the sound bank selected.

GM has opened the door to a thriving industry in prerecorded musical sequences available as Standard MIDI Files on floppy disk. Before GM, this was almost impossible since the makers of commercial sequences would have no idea of the equipment used for playback of the music. Now with a standard, MIDI sequences will sound virtually the same on all systems.

Why buy music in the form of prerecorded MIDI sequences instead of just getting a CD or cassette? Clearly these are entirely different markets. GM doesn't replace an artist's performance on record. However, if you are interested in hearing and then rearranging well-known music on your own music

system, then GM is for you. MIDI sequences are available for most every style, from classical to rock. Sequences for playback on a GM synthesizer adhere to the Standard MIDI File format for playback on many compatible sequencers.

If you sing or play a musical instrument (and if you're reading this you probably do), then having prerecorded music sequences with which you can play along can be fun and educational. Singers can use a GM synthesizer and MIDI sequence as an entire backup band. Unlike an audio recording, the tempo and key for the music can be selected to best fit your vocal range and musical taste. Songs can be entirely rearranged to accommodate for extra lyrics and extended instrumental solos, or shortened to fit into a specific time slot.

Even as just a tool for rehearsal and practice, GM sequences can help any musician prepare for a performance. Getting together with a band to rehearse regularly is difficult. Learning and memorizing your part or lyrics, or practicing a particularly intricate song in privacy will, no doubt, make everybody involved much happier.

GM is also very useful as an educational tool. For example, jazz students have often relied on method books that come with an accompaniment audio recording. With a GM MIDI sequence, the student can practice difficult chord patterns in as slow a tempo as desired until ready to move on. Of course, they can also select any key for practice right from the sequencer.

GM ON THE PERSONAL COMPUTER

Perhaps the most exciting field where GM has had an impact is with personal computers. The market for computer *sound cards* (a special electronic card that fits into an internal slot in a computer) has become enormous, primarily for video game sound enhancement. These cards provide sound capabilities far beyond what is built into most standard PCs. In order for game designers to take advantage of better sounds for their scores, they must know exactly what card the game will use. The industry standard in the IBM world has been the *SoundBlaster* series from Creative Labs for many years. The original was a simple, 11 voice synthesizer with relatively crude sound quality and basic sample playback for sound effects. The newer *SoundBlaster* versions come with many more voices and much better sound quality. Virtually every video game for the IBM PC supports these cards for enhanced sound capabilities.

With the introduction of GM, computer–game software companies recognized that the far superior sound quality and musical sophistication of these instruments were a much desired upgrade from the current crop of relatively simple sound cards. GM-compatible synthesizer cards that plug inside a PC are available from several companies. Many games offer the option of either SoundBlaster or General

General MIDI lets you easily share music with your friends!

MIDI. Of course, while the music and sound effects for games using the SoundBlaster will work with only that one card, games using GM can use any GM synthesizer. Creative Labs released a GM add-on for the SoundBlaster called the *WaveBlaster*.

Games that can support GM instruments can either use an internal card, or can send MIDI to any stand alone GM instrument via any MIDI interface. Many GM synthesizers have built-in computer interfaces that require no additional MIDI hardware to connect to a computer. Some, in fact, provide GM sounds for your computer *and* a MIDI interface for other standard MIDI synthesizers, for the best of both worlds.

Games are not the only use for GM in the computer world. *Multimedia* computing has become an important way for people to share information and make presentations. Multimedia combines pictures, video, animation, sound and text all on a single computer screen. It is used for educational software for both home and classroom, informational kiosks in malls and stores, training systems for company employees and more sophisticated entertainment software for the home computer.

While some multimedia systems rely only on digitally recorded sound from disk, MIDI sequences sent to a GM synthesizer module have become an attractive alternative for some software makers. Recording to hard disks takes up a huge amount of space, while even a very complex MIDI sequence takes up very little space and still sounds great. The use of GM-compatible MIDI Sequences and the proper hardware can allow for hours instead of minutes of music on a small disk. MIDI can also be used to supplement audio recordings in a multimedia presentation.

SUMMARY

General MIDI was added to the MIDI specification in 1990, and gained rapid acceptance and use. GM helps to bring together the more professional musician's world of MIDI sequencers and synthesizers with the more consumer-oriented world of entertainment and home computing. It has also made it technically possible to create and market music in a unique format that can be bent and molded to the users' wishes. With GM instruments, people who wish to collaborate with each other on a musical piece, or simply share their music can exchange a sequence from one studio to another, simply with a disk.

15

Buying MIDI Instruments

Now that you've read about all the fun you could have with a MIDI studio of your own, you're probably itching to run out and put it together. But wait! Here is a top 10 list of helpful tips on what to look for when starting, or adding to, your own MIDI music system:

1

Decide upon your needs and establish a budget. A MIDI system can be made up of MIDI instruments such as synthesizers, rhythm machines, and a sequencer, as well as a mixer, an amplifier, speakers, audio signal processors, a tape recorder, a synchronizer, and the cables to connect everything together. You will probably not need all of these devices (at least not at first), so it is important to know which you do need in order to produce the kind of music you want.

2

Buy a little at a time. Learn an instrument or two at a time before going on to the next one. If you are unhappy with an instrument, you may wish to return, exchange, or sell it before adding another one to your system.

3

Spend some time with each instrument you plan to buy to be sure it has the features and sound you want. For instance, if you are a pianist, you may want an instrument with a more heavily weighted keyboard action and greater polyphony. It is not always possible to return an expensive synthesizer. If you are a composer or songwriter, you may want the versatility of a multitimbral synthesizer or workstation. If you are interested in scoring for video games or multimedia computer software, you should check out the available General MIDI instruments.

Most importantly, be sure you love the sounds of the synthesizer or drum machine you are planning to buy. Since different instruments use a variety of synthesis techniques, each will have a unique sonic personality. Find the ones that feel like they can best express the music you want to make. Don't feel rushed to make a decision. Spend the time at the store playing all the instruments in your price range to be certain you're making the right choice. Although General MIDI synthesizers are all musically compatible, they each have their own sound, and can vary in quality greatly.

4

Look through the instrument's manual before buying. Unfortunately, not all owner's manuals are created equal. Some appear to have been written by crazed, techno-babbling rocket scientists who have never seen a MIDI instrument. For some more popular instruments, there are decent manuals written by outside publishers to supplement the original. Be sure that you can learn how to use your new toy.

Check that the instrument does what you need it to do. Does it have enough polyphony? Is it easy to program? Does it have sliders for sending any MIDI controllers? Can the sequencer lock to tape directly?

5

Ask a lot of questions at the store. Part of what you pay for when you purchase equipment is service and support from the store at which you are buying. The store personnel should be able to answer your questions or find the answers for you. If possible, get to know one salesperson at the store, and do all your purchases through him or her. Loyalty is often rewarded with better discounts and service. After you have made a purchase, you should be able to call your salesperson for any assistance.

Look at the MIDI implementation chart of the instrument in the back of the manual. Every MIDI instrument comes with a guide that shows exactly what the instrument's MIDI capabilities are. The charts are in the same format for every instrument. It will tell you what messages are sent or recognized at a glance.

If you have questions that neither the salesperson nor the manual can answer, have the store call the manufacturer. You deserve to have all your questions answered thoroughly. A salesperson at a store can't know every answer about every product they sell, but it is his or her responsibility to be certain that you get your questions or problems taken care of. Occasionally, a salesperson may make claims about an instrument's capability that may stretch the truth, or be a guess. If you aren't getting all the information you need to make the purchase, don't hesitate to request that the manufacturer be called to confirm an "I think so" or "it should" by the salesperson.

Get a MIDI Thru box or MIDI Patchbay to simplify your larger setup. As your MIDI system grows in size, using the MIDI THRUs provided on each instrument becomes less and less desirable. A *MIDI splitter* or "thru box" is an inexpensive and efficient way to clean up the "mess" of chained MIDI cables. If you are using a patch editor/librarian with your computer, you will need to select different instrument's MIDI OUTs to be sent to the MIDI IN of your computer interface. A *MIDI patchbay* will make the system work without needing to repatch the MIDI connections.

It's better to save a little longer and get the one thing you want, than to buy now and get three things you won't like next month. The best things in life may be free, but musical gear can get expensive. It is important to get the most for your money. While the points above are presented to help you make the best decisions, it also is worth mentioning that the instrument you really want may not be the cheapest one in the store (in fact, it never is). This may be especially true for the bigger items in your studio, such as a MIDI master controller, multitrack tape recorder or mixer.

10

If you are buying a computer and MIDI software, consider the following:

■ Contrary to what many people may say, there is no one best computer for your studio. The main computers for which there is a good supply of music software are the Apple Macintosh, the IBM PC (and other PC compatibles), Atari computers, and, to a lesser degree, the Commodore Amiga. If you plan to collaborate with a partner, you both may want to have the same computer and software, though this isn't absolutely necessary.

■ There is a wide price range for computers. It's difficult to compare different brands since they have different specifications.

■ If you don't yet own a computer, you might want to look at the available MIDI software and buy the computer in your price range that runs the programs you like the best.

■ Most computers come with a modest amount of memory (RAM), and will probably need to be expanded to run certain music software.

■ If you are buying software for a computer you already own, be sure it will work on your system.

■ If you are planning on buying a PC compatible computer or a laptop computer, check that it will handle running MIDI software.

■ Be sure to get the right MIDI interface for your machine. Except for the Atari line of computers, which have built-in MIDI ports, computers do not automatically connect to MIDI, a special interface is necessary. There are several interfaces on the market for each computer. Not all software is compatible will every available MIDI interface. Some MIDI interfaces provide multiple MIDI INs and OUTs to support greater than 16 channels, and have SMPTE In and Out for direct tape synchronization.

■ Sit down and try the program before you buy, or at least read the manual in its entirety. Most music stores have a "no return" policy for MIDI software.

■ Check that the manufacturer has a reasonable policy for obtaining future updates as they become available, and for getting backup disks if the program is copy-protected (not copyable).

Buying the right equipment is a critical step towards having a good musical environment in which to work. The people at the store are there, of course, to sell equipment. By being demanding about information and service, you will have a better chance of getting the goods and services you desire. The purchase of a musical instrument does not begin and end with the item in the box. It includes a relationship with both the company that made it and the people who sold it to you.

Another way to insure that you are making the right choice is by talking to people who already own the equipment you are considering buying. Ask friends, or the store from which you will be buying, to put you in touch with an owner of that equipment. This can be very helpful for both hardware and software purchases.

Buying MIDI equipment should not be a shot in the dark, nor should it be a grueling experience leaving you with horror stories to tell friends. It should be a thoughtful, simple and fulfilling task that provides you with the tools you need to expand your creativity.

Your local music store is a great place to try out new instruments!

16

Problem Solving

Although MIDI is simple and straightforward, problems with it do come up occasionally. Not all MIDI instruments are perfect or easily understood. Sometimes a simple mistake can make people wonder if they are going crazy when nothing works the way it should. While it isn't possible to cover every problem that can occur when setting up and using a MIDI system, here are a few of the more common pitfalls and misunderstandings that happen with MIDI:

"I have connected two MIDI instruments, but when I play on the master, the other synth doesn't make a sound."

This could be due to one or a number of possible reasons:

The audio output of the receiver is not connected or is not turned up. Check the audio cables, mixer and amplifier. Make sure the volume control on the receiving instrument is turned up as well.

■ MIDI OUT of the master is not connected to MIDI IN on the receiver. Check the MIDI cables to be sure they are there and are connected to the right ports.

■ The receiver is set to a different MIDI channel than the master. Check both instruments to see that they are set to the same MIDI channel.

■ If the master controller runs through a sequencer before the receiver, check that the sequencer is set to MIDI THRU On, and the channel is correct.

■ If you have a slider to send MIDI Volume (Controller #7), be sure you haven't sent a Volume message of 0.

"I have one synthesizer and a sequencer. I recorded a bass part into my sequencer and then set the synthesizer to play a flute part for an overdub. When I played back the sequence, the bass part sounded terrible."

■ Unless you are using a multitimbral instrument, you are playing both parts on the flute sound now. A sequencer has no way of knowing the sound a synthesizer is making. You need to keep track of that, and be sure not to use the same synth channel for more than one timbre at a time.

■ If the instrument is multitimbral, then each part will have its own MIDI channel. When overdubbing additional parts into the sequencer, be sure to set the outgoing channel to the matching MIDI channel on the synthesizer with the desired sound.

"My drum machine doesn't start when my sequencer does."

■ Be sure that you have MIDI OUT of the sequencer going to MIDI IN of the drum machine.

■ Check that your sequencer is sending MIDI Clock to the drum machines.

■ Be sure the drum machine is set to play and is in MIDI Sync mode.

"When I play on the master, everything plays, including the drums in the drum machine."

■ Check to see if any of your instruments are set to Omni On mode.

■ Be sure the master isn't sending on several channels at once.

"I have sequenced a few tracks and the parts are starting to sound funny; notes are very short and not the way I played them."

■ You are probably running out of voices on your synthesizer.

■ If you have several tracks on your sequencer all on the same MIDI channel going to one synthesizer, be sure you don't have conflicting pedals or other controllers.

"I was changing MIDI channels from my main keyboard to listen to sounds on different synthesizers. As I was playing, notes would stick sometimes, and I couldn't shut them off!"

■ A note is made up of two separate MIDI *messages*: a Note On and a Note Off. When a key is pressed, the Note On is sent. If the MIDI channel is changed before the key is released, then the Note Off will be on a different MIDI channel than the Note On, and will be ignored by the first receiving synthesizer. The same will be true of pedals, wheels, or any other controllers. Be sure to release the keys and pedals before changing the channel. If your system has some sort of MIDI "panic" button that releases stuck notes, now is a good time to press it.

"My sequencer claims it can record 50,000 notes, but it seems to run out of memory much sooner than that. Was the company not telling the truth, or am I doing something wrong? Can I do something to increase its capacity?"

■ There's more to MIDI than just notes. MIDI keyboards can put out other information in addition to Note Ons that can eat up a lot of memory. One of the biggest memory users is Channel Aftertouch. Keyboards with Aftertouch often generate these messages, even if the patch itself isn't responding to Aftertouch messages. Aftertouch

output can usually be turned off, if you are not expressly using it.

■ Pitch bend and modulation wheels can also eat up a lot of memory space in a sequencer. If it is important to record a large number of notes in a sequence, be as sparing as possible with continuous controllers.

■ In MIDI, a note is made up of two separate events: a Note On and a Note Off. Some sequencers list the number of *events* they can store, not notes. A sequencer able to record 20,000 events is only capable of recording about 10,000 MIDI notes. This is called marketing.

■ The capacity of a computer-based sequencer is dependent on the amount of memory in the computer. If you are having problems fitting your music into your computer, look into expanding the RAM in the machine.

"Notes are sticking when I play my sequences back."

■ Due to bugs in software, or occasional glitches in a MIDI interface, it is possible that some notes will stick for what seems like no good reason (actually, there *is* no good reason for notes to stick). If the sequencer or interface has a "panic" or "all notes off" feature, press that. Then call the manufacturer and report the problem. If you are running a computer-based sequencer, be sure you are not running too many "goodies" such as desk accessories, system extensions, or added software unnecessary for MIDI.

"My synthesizer claims to have 16 voices of polyphony. Yet I can't play chords with more than 4 notes."

■ Many larger master controller keyboards can send on two or more channels at once. Occasionally, it is possible to accidentally have the keyboard send two or more MIDI events on the same channel for every key press. This will eat up the polyphony of a synthesizer rather quickly.

■ If you are using a sequencer, be sure you have not inadvertently duplicated the data of a track, and are sending multiple events for each desired note.

"Some of my synthesizers aren't responding to Program Changes and Volume messages I'm sending to them."

- Most synthesizers have a set of MIDI message "filters" that instruct the instrument to either respond to, or ignore, incoming MIDI events. Check to see if a Program Change filter is active.

- If you are using a sequencer, check its MIDI message filter to see if it is ignoring Program Change messages.

There's no way to anticipate all of the problems that can arise from using electronic equipment. If all else fails:

- Read the manual

- Call the store that sold it to you

- Call the manufacturer that made it

- Call an authorized repair shop

- Pray

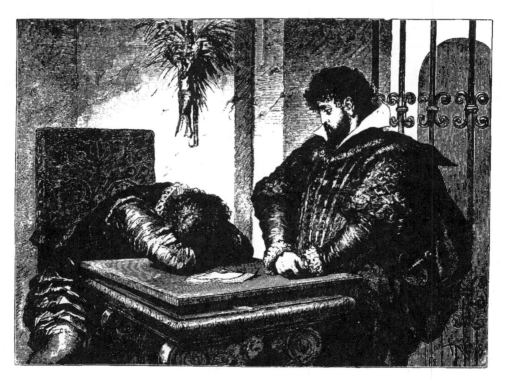

"No, I can't read another manual!"

17

Putting It All Together

It's finally time to look at what makes up a MIDI *system*. With an understanding of the INs, OUTs, and THRUs of MIDI, everything in this chapter should come together for you.

A MIDI system starts with some instruments. You need one as a master controller on which to perform. You also need one or more additional MIDI instruments slaved to the controller for additional parts or sounds. To complete the studio, you will want a sequencer—which can be a stand-alone model or one that runs on your personal computer–and all the audio equipment needed to hear everything. Finally, you'll need one or more people—including yourself—to create, play and listen to music.

BASICS

A MIDI system can be as simple as two instruments connected together with a single MIDI cable (**Figure 17-1**). This could be used in a basic live performance situation.

In this setup, playing on the master keyboard will play both instruments, as long as they are set to the same MIDI channel.

The next level of sophistication would be to add a third instrument or more. This can be done either by using the MIDI THRU port of the first slave instrument, or by using a MIDI *thru box* or *patchbay,* which have one MIDI IN and several MIDI THRUs. This is still a setup for live performance.

- In **Figure 17-2**, MIDI OUT from the master keyboard goes to MIDI IN of the first slave instrument.

- The MIDI THRU of the slave repeats the data from the sender on the second slave instrument.

- Both slaves are set to the same MIDI Channel as the master.

- In **Figure 17-3**, MIDI OUT from the master keyboard goes to MIDI In of a MIDI thru box.

- Each MIDI OUT of the thru box goes to the MIDI IN of a slave instrument.

- All slaves are set to the same MIDI Channel as the master.

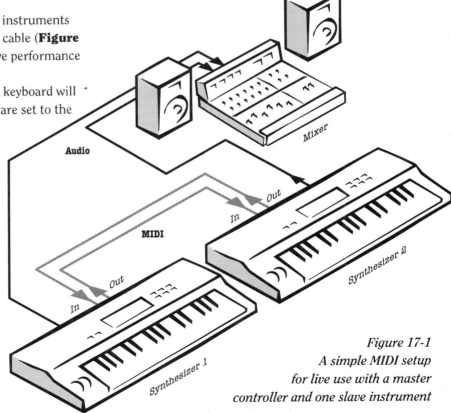

Figure 17-1
A simple MIDI setup
for live use with a master
controller and one slave instrument

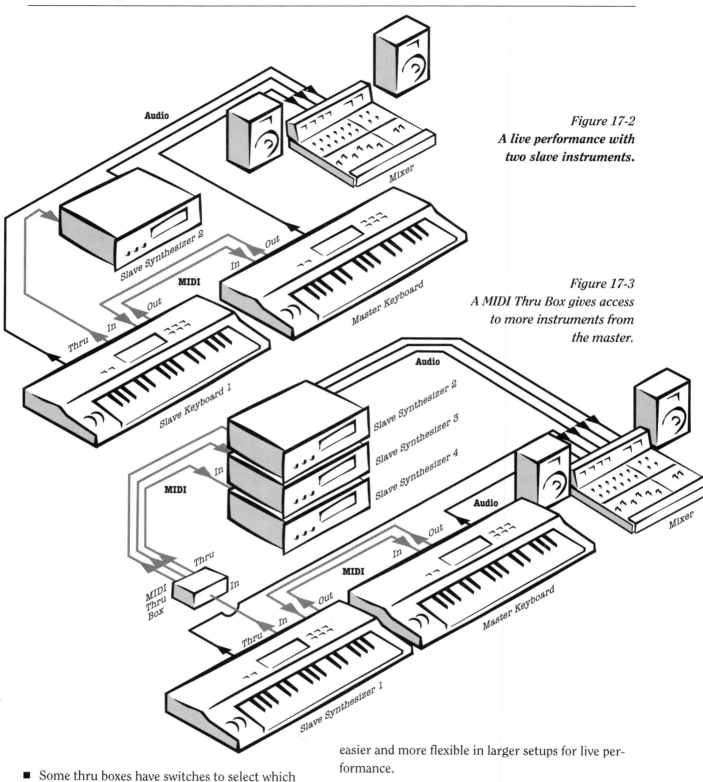

Figure 17-2
***A live performance with
two slave instruments.***

Figure 17-3
***A MIDI Thru Box gives access
to more instruments from
the master.***

■ Some thru boxes have switches to select which MIDI OUTs send MIDI and which do not. This allows for quick selection of sound layers with the various slaves.

Both systems work perfectly well, and there is no real advantage to one or the other. Using a thru box makes it possible to add even more instruments without building a long chain of MIDI THRUs to MIDI INs on the instruments themselves, which is easier and more flexible in larger setups for live performance.

SEQUENCING

For composing and arranging music, no MIDI studio is complete without a sequencer. Here's how to connect a keyboard synthesizer, a sequencer and one or more additional MIDI instruments. **Figure 17-4** illustrates a very typical MIDI system.

■ The MIDI OUT of the keyboard goes to the MIDI IN of the sequencer to send MIDI data to it.

■ The sequencer, with a single MIDI IN and OUT, needs to send data to several destinations. By using a MIDI thru box, the output of the sequencer is split and sent to each receiving instrument's MIDI IN, as well as going back to the master keyboard's MIDI IN for playback.

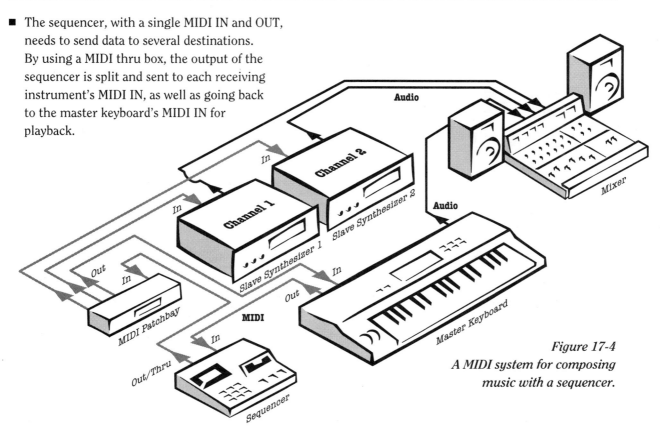

Figure 17-4
A MIDI system for composing
music with a sequencer.

■ When not recording, the sequencer passes all data from its MIDI IN to its MIDI OUT port. Most sequencers can change the MIDI Channel of the incoming data in order to direct it to the desired slave instrument set to that same channel. Doing so lets you preview each part on the synthesizer of your choice from the master controller.

Multitimbral synthesizers are used like any other MIDI instrument, only now a single box is capable of performing many parts by responding to many MIDI Channels at a time.

The setup is the same, only you reserve a set of channels for each instrument, as shown in **Figure 17-5**. It's important to be careful that channels don't overlap between the machines, or you'll have parts played by multiple instruments unintentionally.

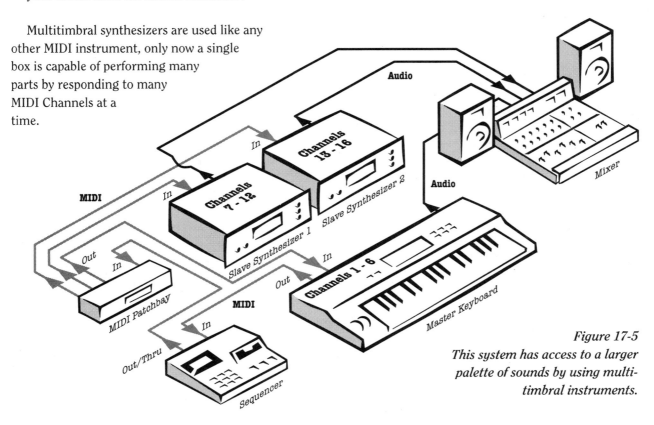

Figure 17-5
This system has access to a larger
palette of sounds by using multi-
timbral instruments.

With the addition of a sequencer, a drum machine may not be far behind (unless you are far behind on the payments for your sequencer). The setup will be something like **Figure 17-6**.

MIDI drum machines can be used in one of two ways: with the drum part programmed into it and synchronized to the main sequencer, or as a MIDI sound module

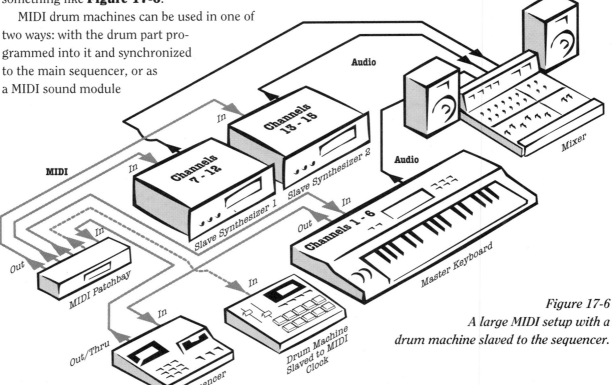

Figure 17-6
A large MIDI setup with a
drum machine slaved to the sequencer.

with the drum parts recorded into the main sequencer along with the rest of the music. In the first case, the following occurs:

- The main sequencer transmits MIDI Clocks based on the tempo you've set.

- The drum machine's MIDI IN is connected to the MIDI OUT of the sequencer, and will synchronize its performance to those Clocks.

- The drum machine is set to MIDI Sync Mode, as opposed to Internal Sync Mode. This slaves its performance to the master sequencer.

- Once the machine is connected and set to the proper mode, the master sequencer will run the drum machine via MIDI—you need not touch the drum machine to start or stop it.

- Be sure that the MIDI Channel of the drum machine isn't the same as another slave synthesizer, or you'll get extra notes being played on the drums.

Programming rhythms on a drum machine is, for many people, easier and more intuitive than using a keyboard and sequencer. The pads used for triggering the drums are better organized than tapping keys on a piano-style keyboard. The looping method of sequencing used by drum machines makes creating and editing each rhythm easier than most sequencers. In many cases, the rhythmic accuracy of drum machines is superior to a standard MIDI sequencer. In short, the MIDI drum machine has been optimized for doing one thing well—recording and organizing drum and percussion parts for songs.

However, drum machines can also act as MIDI sound modules, responding to Note On information from an external source. The drum parts are played from a MIDI keyboard or MIDI drum kit, recorded into a sequencer, and played back on the drum machine's sampled sounds. Because the drum parts get recorded and stored along with the rest of the music in the master sequencer's memory, this has some advantages over using a drum machine's sequencer. If you choose to remove, add or rearrange some measures in the song, you only have to do so once. With a drum machine programmed and slaved to the main sequencer, you would have to perform the edit twice.

When using a drum machine simply as a sound module, do not put it into MIDI Sync Mode, since you don't want to start playback on its own sequencer. The drum machine is being used only as a sound source. There are also a number of MIDI drum modules with no built-in sequencing capabilities.

A MIDI drum machine assigns a MIDI note number to each of its internal drum sounds. By hitting the proper key on a MIDI keyboard, the corresponding drum will sound. A look in the owner's manual of a MIDI drum machine will show you how the drum sounds are mapped to key numbers and how to change them to suit your own tastes and style.

A drum module fits into a MIDI system just as any other MIDI synthesizer, as shown in **Figure 17-7**.

Figure 17-7
A large MIDI system
including a drum machine
receiving note messages.

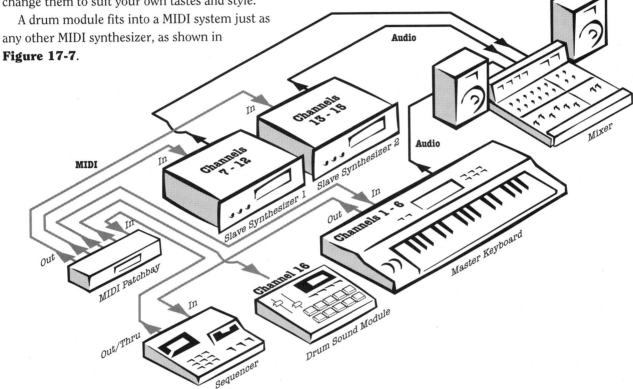

MIDI PATCHBAYS

If you own a number of synthesizers and use a computer both for sequencing and organizing your sounds, then you run into the problem of how to get Sysex data from each instrument into the computer. There is a simple answer to that problem, and it is to use a *MIDI patchbay* to selectively route MIDI from each synth only as needed for the librarian program. You'll never need to touch a cable again.

As the sophistication of your music systems grows, the necessity for organizing the connection between the various components becomes more and more apparent. Recording studios, for example, require an enormous amount of audio equipment, each piece having inputs and outputs. It is often necessary to change the way components are connected:

the output of a tape track may need to go to a mixer at one point and to a delay device next. A microphone can be connected to an input channel of the mixer, to a compressor, or to a special effects device. This is called *patching*. As a musical situation changes, so does the patching of the system.

So, add a *MIDI patchbay* to the list of MIDI devices you might require. If you have just one or two MIDI instruments, or do not use a patch librarian, a MIDI patchbay is not essential. However, if you find it necessary to change MIDI cables in order to perform different tasks, these devices are definite time-savers.

A typical MIDI patchbay (see **Figure 17-8**) has several MIDI INs and MIDI OUTs. By using controls on the patchbay's front panel, it can route any IN to any OUT. A patchbay may also have memories, so that various routing setups can be stored for recall later. Many patchbays will respond to MIDI Program Change messages to change from one setup to another. Some patchbays are able to merge two or more INs to the same OUT. It is also possible to route one input go to several outputs in order to split the MIDI information like a simple MIDI thru box.

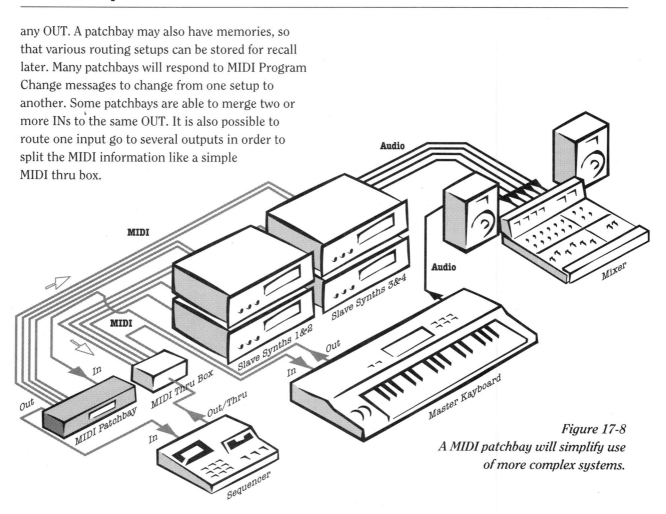

Figure 17-8
A MIDI patchbay will simplify use of more complex systems.

MIDI patchbays are highly recommended in a MIDI system with a patch librarian and a personal computer. Most sequencer or computer MIDI interfaces have only a single MIDI IN port. That precious input is needed most of the time by the master keyboard. If you need to do a System Exclusive data transmission from a synthesizer module instrument into the patch librarian program, you would have to unplug the keyboard in order to connect the other instrument, then put everything back to resume sequencing. A patchbay solves this problem by allowing you to choose the way all the MIDI messages will be routed for a given application.

Some more sophisticated computer MIDI interfaces have multiple MIDI IN and OUT ports. This is a tremendous jump in power for a studio, since you can go far beyond the limit of 16 MIDI channels, and thus 16 musical parts. It also eliminates the need for a separate MIDI patchbay, since all the capabilities of a patchbay are built right into the interface. With one multi-port interface, you can connect the MIDI INs and OUTs of every piece of gear in your studio to the computer at once. Any sequencer or patch librarian program you use must be specially made to support the interface, in order to get the benefit of the multiple ports.

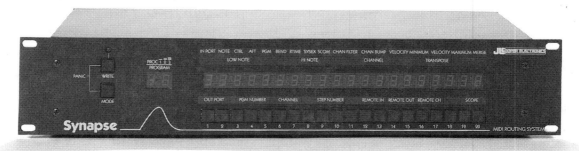

Figure 17-9
A MIDI patchbay's front panel.

The benefit of a multi-port interface for sequencing is having access to more channels on more instruments. Each port on the interface will support 16 channels. When using a patch editor or librarian, you can receive MIDI Sysex back from each

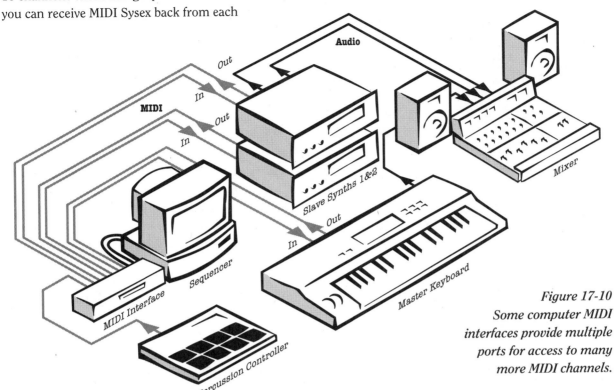

Figure 17-10
Some computer MIDI interfaces provide multiple ports for access to many more MIDI channels.

synthesizer without changing MIDI cables. One setup suits all your needs.

Figure 17-10 shows how a studio is setup around a computer-based sequencer and a multi-port MIDI interface:

SYNCHRONIZING TO TAPE

Synthesizers don't replace the need for recording live parts onto audio tape on occasion. If you are a songwriter, you will want to record lead and background vocals. Almost any type of music benefits from the addition of some "real" instruments or voices. The wonderful thing about working with MIDI sequencers and multitrack tape is that the synthesizer parts never have to be recorded to the tape. Sequencers and tape can be *synchronized* together, so MIDI parts are in the sequencer and acoustic parts are on multitrack tape, both working together as one. When finished, the whole piece can be mixed and recorded to a stereo master tape. Welcome to the "virtual studio."

Most sequencers, computer MIDI interfaces, and drum machines have built-in *sync to tape*. Tape sync

is a special audio signal created by a MIDI device that is recorded onto one track of the multitrack tape and then played back into the device. It's simple to use. The sequencer can record or playback while locked to the sync signal tape.

All sequencers and drum machines have special timing clocks that maintain the tempo to which you set them. Tape sync converts this clock into tones that are recorded onto tape as shown in **Figure 17-11**. The sync signal is usually labeled *sync out* or *tape out* on most devices.

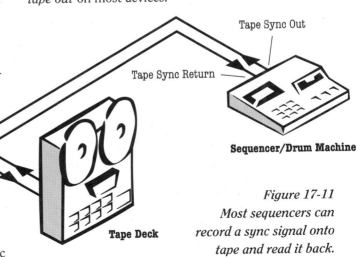

Figure 17-11
Most sequencers can record a sync signal onto tape and read it back.

Three technologies are available for synchronizing sequencers to tape. Virtually every sequencer or special tape synchronizer uses one of these:

- FSK (Frequency Shifted Keying)

- Smart FSK (with Song Position Pointer capabilities)

- SMPTE Time Code

The FSK tone has been around the longest, and is the least used now. An FSK tone is generated by a sequencer or other tape synchronizer, and is recorded onto one track of a multitrack tape. The tone contains little pulses at the current tempo of the device. In order to lock to the tape, the tempo of the music must be selected prior to recording any audio. Then the sync tone is recorded onto a track of the tape. The *sync track* is then fed back to the sequencer or sync device. Next, the sequencer is set to a Tape Sync Mode, which makes it look at the tape for a tempo and start time. Upon playing the tape, the sync tone is used by the sequencer as the master clock for tempo. Once the sync tone is recorded, the tempo can not be changed without redoing it.

Another problem with working with FSK is that you must start the music from the beginning every time you synchronize with the tape. That problem is fixed with *smart FSK*. It works in the same manner as standard (or shall we call it "dumb"?) FSK, but it provides for starting and working from the middle of a MIDI sequence. In addition to encoding the music's tempo, smart FSK blends in a steady stream of MIDI Song Position Pointer messages directly onto the tape. Upon playback, the sync tone sends back the current song position from the current spot on the tape to the sequencer, which

quickly locates to the same point in the sequence and begins playing at the proper tempo. Smart FSK is usually found in stand alone synchronizer boxes that are used in conjunction with a sequencer.

Since the speed of most tape machines fluctuates slightly, so does the sync tone being sent back to the sequencer. In turn, the sequencer, which is using the tone as its own master clock, also adjusts to keep pace with the tape. The end result is that the speed of the sequencer is perfectly synchronized to the speed of the tape.

Using a multitrack recorder, even the most basic four-track cassette studio, gives more power to any MIDI system. In addition to recording voices or other instruments, you can also synchronize and overdub your synthesizers onto tape, which effectively gives you the sound of many more instruments than you actually have. If there are more parts in your music than you have instruments available, a few parts can be recorded at a time on each track of the tape machine by synchronizing the sequencer. You can also take advantage of layering several instruments onto a track of the tape for a single part to get a bigger, lusher sound.

Tape synchronization is not available on every sequencer or drum machine. When it is not, you need a separate, stand-alone synchronizer.

SMPTE—MIDI, FILM, AND VIDEO

The third technique for synchronization is the use of SMPTE time code, as described in *Chapter 10*.

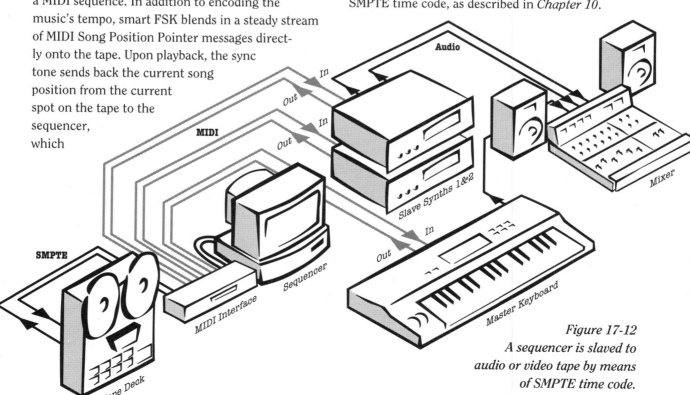

Figure 17-12
A sequencer is slaved to audio or video tape by means of SMPTE time code.

SMPTE was originally developed for the synchronization of video and audio recording machines. It is extremely flexible and accurate, and is required for anyone composing music for film or television. SMPTE time code, referred to simply as *time code*, has in fact become the standard for all professional synchronization tasks in recording studios, film and television production facilities throughout most of the world. Europe uses a slightly different standard, called *EBU time code*, but it is used in the exact same way as the SMPTE time code.

Time code is recorded on tape as an audio signal, the same as FSK sync. A major advantage of using time code over FSK or smart FSK is that the tempo of the music is not recorded to the sync track of the tape. Instead, time code records *real time* onto the tape. Real time means that time is divided into hours, minutes, and seconds, just like any normal clock. SMPTE time code measures time the same as any clock. However, in order to be more accurate, SMPTE time goes beyond seconds in accuracy, adding *frames* and *bits*. Frames are used as a reference because SMPTE time code was developed to count frames numbers on video tape. There are thirty frames in a second and eighty bits in each frame. This provides an impressive timing accuracy of .0004 of a second.

Time code is generated by all the computer MIDI interfaces that offer a tape sync feature. They generate the code to go to tape, read the code back from tape, and convert the time code to MIDI Time Code (MTC), which can be sent via MIDI to the sequencer. SMPTE time code is also found on a number of stand-alone drum machines and sequencers as well.

The music's tempos remain in the sequencer. When the time code is received, the interface reads the current position of the tape by the current SMPTE time. In this type of sync system, the tempo is accurate, flexible, and adjustable. Unlike with FSK, an overdubbed synthesizer part for a multitrack recording that feels early or late to music on the tape can be adjusted early or late to match the rest of the tracks by having the sequencer begin a frame or two earlier or later.

Since SMPTE time code does not contain tempo, it is possible to record a sync tone first, and change your mind about tempo later. This is impossible to do with an FSK track. **Figure 17-12** shows how a computer-based sequencer with SMPTE time code capabilities is integrated into a MIDI system.

There are also stand alone *synchronizers* for recording and reading SMPTE time code, and converting it to either MTC or MIDI Real Time messages to send to a sequencer. Those able to send Real Time messages contain *tempo maps* (a list of tempo changes) in their memories, so the sequencer's tempo or tempos are not used. The connection is shown in **Figure 17-13**. These synchronizers merge MIDI from a master controller with its own Real Time messages in order to allow you to record MIDI parts into the sequencer while locked to tape.

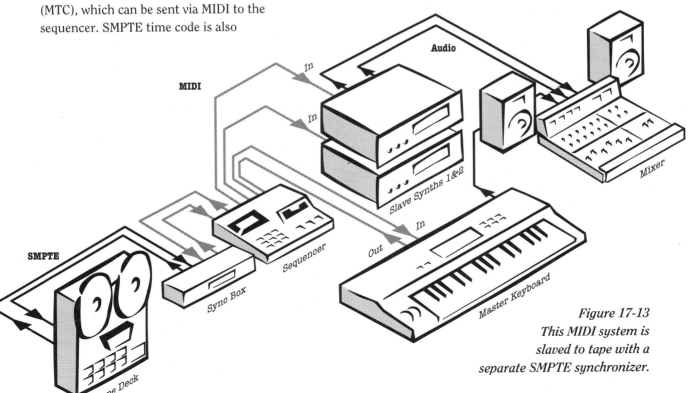

Figure 17-13
This MIDI system is
slaved to tape with a
separate SMPTE synchronizer.

There is almost no end to the wonderful devices, instruments, controllers, processors and synchronizers that can be added to a music studio. Putting together a great MIDI system involves deciding just what your personal musical needs are, and assembling the most flexible system to satisfy them. With a bit of knowledge and common sense, most MIDI systems are very simple to design and fun to use. The diagrams in this chapter are good examples of some of the ways in which a typical MIDI system is put together.

As you start or add to your own MIDI system, the logic of MIDI's flow and abilities becomes clearer and clearer. MIDI can be adapted to just about any musical situation without the need for odd kludges or weird gizmos. The best system for you is based on the type of music you make, the equipment you have or want, your budget, and the way you feel most comfortable making music.

FINAL CONCLUSIONS

Now that you've gotten a glimpse into the internal workings of one of the great phenomena of modern music making, it might be worthwhile to look at the importance of all this information. Certainly a musician doesn't need to know how to build a synthesizer in order to play it, just as you don't need to know how cars work in order to drive one. Why then is it important to understand so much about MIDI?

MIDI instruments, by their power and ease of use, provide a source of great inspiration to musicians and composers. Working with older, pre-MIDI electronic instruments was difficult and slow. MIDI's simplicity and flexibility makes it possible to experiment with different sounds and musical ideas very quickly. MIDI has enhanced tremendously the cre-

ative process when working with electronic instruments, by making them easier to learn, easier to use, more powerful, and much more fun.

Along with this conceptual simplicity comes some new complexity, however. MIDI provides you with a *personal music system*, with a lot of options to consider, and equipment to learn. To design and use a personal music system to its maximum capability does indeed require an understanding of all the components, as well as a solid grasp of MIDI's INs, OUTs, and THRUs.

For example, editing individual MIDI events, or inserting a MIDI controller message into a track on a sequencer will be frustrating or useless to the musician that doesn't have a knowledge of what MIDI looks like and does. It really helps to know what MIDI messages exist, what their codes look like, and what they all do in order to use them most successfully. The more you know, the more creative you can be with the tools at hand. Just like playing any musical instrument, the more technically accomplished you are, more expressive you can be with it.

MIDI is a tool, and like most any other tool, does not replace anything else. It has a role to play in your creative process. It helps to keep a certain perspective in mind when putting a MIDI system together, or using your studio to make music. It is that MIDI is just one available tool. Technique, musicianship, creativity, and a bit of common sense are others that also go into making good music. If you are building a house you would use a hammer, but you won't built a house *out of hammers*. It's the same with MIDI. It is one tool to be mastered and used with all the others to build music that is expressive and accomplished. Enjoy.

Artistic freedom is within your grasp!

A1

Appendix 1:
Computer Counting Systems

COMPUTER COUNTING SYSTEMS

While a knowledge of computer theory and mathematics is not necessary to use MIDI to its fullest, understanding MIDI's digital roots can help understand some of the logic behind it.

BINARY AND HEXADECIMAL

Since the people who invented computers were mathematicians, they were more comfortable thinking of the bits of digital memory as being either 0 or 1 instead of being *on* or *off*, which is in fact a more accurate description. The two numerical values for a single bit, 1 and 0, are used by all computer programmers. While this is one of the great technical accomplishments of the Twentieth Century, being able to count up to only 1 is not very useful.

To remedy this problem, the bits are combined into groups to represent larger numbers. These groups are called *bytes*, and they are like numbers with more than one digit in them. In MIDI, a byte is a group of eight bits, and can represent numerical values from 0 to 255. This is called *binary arithmetic*. In binary math, each column is *twice* the numerical value of the column to its right, just as in the standard *decimal* math, each column is *ten* times the numerical value of the column to its right. The mathematical numbering system used in eight-bit computers and MIDI is called *hexadecimal*. It is a standard for computer systems. In hexademical math, each column is *sixteen* times the numerical value of the column to its right. **Figure A-1** shows the value of each column in binary, decimal and hexadecimal arithmetic.

There are ten digits, 0 to 9, in our standard *decimal* numbering system, also called *base ten arithmetic*. Hexadecimal is also called *base sixteen arithmetic*. There are sixteen different digits in hexadecimal. The letters A to F are used to represent the digits above 9.

Here is a chart showing the relationship between decimal and hexadecimal counting:

Decimal	Hexadecimal	Decimal	Hexadecimal
0	00	16	10
1	00	17	11
2	02	18	12
3	03	19	13
4	04	20	14
5	05	21	15
6	06	22	16
7	07	23	17
8	08	24	18
9	09	25	19
10	0A	26	1A
11	0B	27	1B
12	0C	28	1C
13	0D	29	1D
14	0E	30	1E
15	0F	31	1F

Figure A-2 Decimal and Hexadecimal compared.

Figure A-2 shows the first thirty two digits of the hexadecimal counting system. It is common in technical documents to place a zero in front of a single-digit hexadecimal number, and an "H" (for "hexadecimal") after it.

A two digit hexadecimal number can represent any eight bit value. The first digit represents the first four bits, and the second digit represents the second four bits. Notice in **Figure A-1** that by adding the values of the first four binary columns together you get the number 15. Since numbers start from zero, that means there are 16 possible values in four bits, the same as can be represented

Column	8	7	6	5	4	3	2	1
Binary	128	64	32	16	8	4	2	1
Decimal	10,000,000	1,000,000	100,000	10,000	1,000	100	10	1
Hexadecimal	268,435,456	16,777,216	1,048,576	65,536	4,096	256	16	1

Figure A-1 The value of numeric columns in various counting systems.

by a single hexadecimal digit. Thus two hexadecimal digits represent all eight bits in the MIDI protocol.

MIDI instruments distinguish status and data messages by the "top" or eighth bit. If it is a 1, then the message is status. If it is a 0, then it is data. This means that all data messages have only seven available bits. If you add together the values of the lower seven binary values, you get 127. This is why all MIDI data messages are within the range of 0 to 127. In hexadecimal, 127 is 7FH, and in binary it is 0111 1111. The next higher value is, respectively 128, 80H, or 1000 0000. Now the "top" bit is a 1, and it is the first available status message, which is Note Off on Channel 1.

Channels in MIDI are represented in the lower four bits of every MIDI status message. It is possible to show which channel a MIDI message is on with a *single* hexadecimal digit, because they have sixteen possible values (**Figure A-3**).

So by showing a MIDI byte in hexadecimal, you can easily see the channel number by looking at its lower digit. MIDI instruments display the first Channel as number 1, not 0. Thus, the actual MIDI Channel number is one higher than the hexadecimal code number transmitted over MIDI.

As an example, the MIDI code for a Note On event on Channel 1 is 90H. The first digit, the 9, is the MIDI code for a Note On. The second digit, the 0, is the MIDI channel, which is set to Channel 1. A Note On on MIDI Channel 2 would be 91H, a Note On on MIDI Channel 3 would be 92H, and so on. So a MIDI status byte that is displayed in hexadecimal can be split into two parts, the type of message represented in the first digit and the channel number represented in the second digit.

There is a standard way of writing a MIDI status message without its channel, if the channel is not important. For example, if a Note On message is shown, but the channel is not important, it will be written as "9n." The lowercase "n" takes the place of the channel number. In fact "n" stands for "number." When you see this in a MIDI technical document or instrument owners manual, it simply means "a Note On on any MIDI channel."

Parts of many MIDI documents use hexadecimal numbers. The MIDI Detailed Specification, the bible of the MIDI protocol, lists all MIDI messages in hexadecimal and binary. Many of the manuals that accompany MIDI instruments will list all the MIDI messages and Sysex formats in hexadecimal form. Knowing a little of MIDI mathematical basis makes reading these charts a bit less cryptic.

Hexadecimal	Binary	Decimal	MIDI Channel
00	0000	0	Channel 1
01	0001	1	Channel 2
02	0010	2	Channel 3
03	0011	3	Channel 4
04	0100	4	Channel 5
05	0101	5	Channel 6
06	0110	6	Channel 7
07	0111	7	Channel 8
08	1000	8	Channel 9
09	1001	9	Channel 10
0A	1010	10	Channel 11
0B	1011	11	Channel 12
0C	1100	12	Channel 13
0D	1101	13	Channel 14
0E	1110	14	Channel 15
0F	1111	15	Channel 16

Figure A-3
MIDI Channels can be noted with a single "Hex" digit, or four binary "bits."

A2

Appendix 2: Glossary

Active Sensing: A MIDI message sent by some instruments that tells receiving instruments to shut off during performance in the event that a MIDI cable is disconnected.

Aftertouch (also called *"key pressure"*): A MIDI Continuous Controller message sent by some keyboards when pressure is applied to a key after it has been struck.

AM: See *Amplitude Modulation*.

amplitude: Volume.

Amplitude Modulation: The periodic changing of *amplitude* (volume) to create expressive effects such as tremolo.

analog: In synthesis, the use of voltages to control the *pitch*, *timbre*, and *amplitude* of a sound.

baud rate: Usually, the speed (in bits per second) at which data travels from device to device. For example, MIDI travels at 31, 250 baud.

binary: The number system used by computers to represent information. Numbers in the binary system can have a value of either 0 or 1 (base 2).

bit: A single *binary* digit stored in a computer device. Bits can have a value of either 0 or 1, forming what is called "binary code" (see *binary*). MIDI sends bits from instrument to instrument in special code combinations.

Breath Controller: A MIDI *Continuous Controller* code generated by a device that is sensitive to air pressure. It is used by placing the device in the mouth and blowing. The breath controller is usually used to produce modulation.

Bulk Dump: In MIDI, the transmission of the entire contents of an instrument's memory via *System Exclusive* to another compatible instrument or to a computer.

buss: The part of a mixer that sends the sound from an audio source to specific tracks on the tape during recording.

byte: A group of eight *bits*. *Bits* are arranged in groups of 8 to represent a larger range of numbers. MIDI messages are sent as a series of bytes.

Central Processing Unit (CPU): The part of a computer that runs the software and hardware.

channel: An informational pathway over which MIDI data is transmitted or received. MIDI can transmit or receive information on as many as sixteen *channels* over a single MIDI cable. The lower four *bits* of each MIDI *status byte* indicate the MIDI *channel* for the data that follows. (See Chapter 5)

Channel Key Pressure: A MIDI message sent when a key is pressed down after it has been struck. The value generated by the key that is pressed the hardest is used for the entire MIDI *channel*. Also called *"Aftertouch."*

Channel Mode Messages: See *Mode Messages*.

Channel Number: The lower four *bits* of each MIDI status *byte* that indicate the MIDI *channel* for the data that follows. MIDI instruments only respond to messages on the same *channel* to which they are set.

Channel Voice Messages: The MIDI codes that represent the actual musical performance. These include *Note On* and *Off*, *Pitch Bend*, *Continuous Controllers*, *Program Changes*, and *Aftertouch*.

clock rate: See *resolution*.

code: A system of communication using special symbols or numbers to represent information. MIDI is a code.

Continue: The MIDI message used to tell all clock-based devices, such as *sequencers* and *drum machines*, to play from the point at which they last stopped.

Continuous Controllers: Any of the MIDI codes created by moving wheels, levers, pedals, or sliders. *Modulation wheel* and *breath controllers* are examples of Continuous Controllers.

Control Change: The category of MIDI messages created by *continuous controllers*, switches or pedals.

control voltage: In analog synthesis, the technique of using voltages to represent and control the various parameters of a *synthesizer*.

CV: See control voltage.

data: Information.

data bytes: The *bytes* sent after a MIDI *Status Byte* to define the specific values of information being sent.

delay (also called a "Digital Delay Line" or "DDL"): An audio effects device used to produce echoes and reverberations.

digital: Any technology that uses numbers to represent other forms of information. For example, MIDI uses numbers to represent performance information. Many synthesizers use numbers to create and represent waveforms. CD players and sampling keyboards store sounds as large blocks of numbers, thus all these devices are considered digital.

DIN plug: The standard hardware used for all MIDI connectors.

drum machine: A device that emulates the sounds of drums or percussion and can record and play back rhythm patterns.

effects: Devices that change the characteristics of an audio signal passed through them. Reverb, delay, chorus, flanging, equalization, and panning units are all effects. Sometimes called *audio signal processors*.

envelope: The part of a *synthesizer* used to give contour and shape to an electronic sound.

equalization (EQ): The ability to add or subtract bass and treble from an individual sound.

External Sync: In MIDI, the mode on a sequencer or drum machine in which the device uses incoming *MIDI Timing Clocks* to determine its *tempo*, as well as when it will start and stop playing.

FM: See *Frequency Modulation*.

Frequency Modulation: The periodic changing of frequency to create expressive effects such as *vibrato*. Frequency Modulation (FM) can also be used to create entirely new sounds.

FSK (Frequency Shift Keying): A technique to record clock pulses onto audio tape by using different tones to represent the pulses. FSK is used occasionally to synchronize *sequencers* and *drum machines* to tape.

hexadecimal (also called "*hex*"): A method for representing numbers in base sixteen. Digits 0 to 9 are used along with digits A to F. Hexadecimal numbers are used to make MIDI information easier to read, since there are sixteen unique hexadecimal digits to represent the sixteen MIDI *channels*.

importing: The process of opening a file, such as a *Standard MIDI File*, into a program other than the one in which it was created.

interface: The interconnection of separate devices to create a larger system.

Internal Sync: The mode in which a *sequencer* or *drum machine* uses its own clock to determine tempo.

key number: The numerical value for each key of a MIDI keyboard. MIDI has a range of 128 key numbers (0 to 127).

keyboard controller: The keyboard used to control other synthesizers and samplers in a MIDI studio; also referred to as *mother keyboard*.

keypressure: See *Aftertouch*.

Local Control: A keyboard *synthesizer*'s ability to send MIDI messages without triggering its own sound circuitry.

LSB–Least Significant Byte: A second *data byte* used for increasing the *resolution* of some controllers.

Manufacturer's Identification Number: A number assigned to each manufacturer of MIDI instruments, which is used to identify the company when sending a *System Exclusive* message.

memory: Special chips used by digital devices to retain information such as *patch* parameters or digitally-recorded sound, sometimes referred to as RAM or ROM.

microprocessor: The chip that is the "brain" of any *digital* system. It is capable of manipulating and transmitting data as well as performing mathematical operations at great speeds. Also called a *CPU*.

MIDI: Musical Instrument Digital Interface. A means by which musical performance and other information is transmitted and received by instruments using a common serial *interface*. Also the main topic of this book.

MIDI clock: The MIDI code sent by a *sequencer* or *drum machine* at the rate of 24 times per beat to synchronize the *tempo* of other clock-based MIDI devices in the system.

MIDI Machine Control: A portion of the MIDI specification for the remote control of video and audio tape machines, and other devices.

MIDI Manufacturers Association (MMA): The organization that determines the MIDI standard for the U.S.and Europe.

MIDI Sync: The mode on a *sequencer* or *drum machine* that causes it to start, stop and play at the same *tempo* as a *sequencer/drum machine* connected to it.

MIDI Time Code (MTC): The MIDI messages that represent *SMPTE Time Code*; used for synchronization purposes.

millisecond: 1/1000th (.001) of a second.

Mode: In MIDI, the way in which an instrument will respond to incoming MIDI data. The four MIDI modes are: Omni On/Poly, Omni Off/Poly, Omni On/Mono, and Omni Off/Mono. It is possible to command an instrument to change modes via MIDI.

modem: A device that allows computers to exchange information over telephone lines. The word is a contraction of "MOdulator/DEModulator."

Mode Messages: The MIDI commands used to change the mode of an instrument. These commands tell a MIDI *synthesizer* to receive data in a certain way.

modulation: In synthesis, the periodic changing of a sound's pitch or *amplitude*. *Vibrato* is one form of *frequency modulation*, and tremolo is one form of *amplitude modulation*. See FM and AM.

modulation wheel: The controller on a synthesizer used for sending *modulation*, usually in the form of *vibrato*.

monophonic: The performance of a single note at a time.

mother keyboard: A term used to describe a keyboard that generates MIDI codes to control other instruments. Often called a "MIDI controller" or "master keyboard."

MSB–Most Significant Byte: A single *data byte* that is used to represent the entire numeric range of some *parameter*.

MTC: Stands for both "MIDI Time Code" and "Master Time Code."

multimedia: The combination of pictures, video, animation, sound, and text on a single computer screen.

multi-timbral: The capability of some *synthesizers* to play more than one type of sound or tone color at a time on different MIDI *channels*.

multitrack: A tape recorder that has four or more tracks on which to record.

multitrack recording: An audio recording technique that keeps each musical part discretely on its own area of the tape.

Note Off: The MIDI code that tells an instrument to stop a note that is currently playing. It consists of three *bytes*: the *status byte* (which includes the MIDI *channel*); the key number (what note it is); and the *velocity* (how quickly the note is to be released).

Note On: The MIDI code that commands an instrument to play a note. It consists of three *bytes*: the *status byte* (which includes the MIDI channel); the key number (what note it is); and the *velocity* (how fast the key is hit). Note Ons with a velocity of zero are often used to stop a note that is playing.

Omni: A MIDI mode that determines whether an instrument will respond to one or several MIDI *channels*.

oscillator: In synthesis, special electronic circuits in a *synthesizer* that create the actual sounds.

packet: The combination of a *status byte* and *data bytes* sent together to describe a musical event.

parameter: A single variable in a group. Parameters in a *synthesizer* program would be *waveforms*, filter settings, or envelope profiles. In MIDI, parameters would include the key number in a *Note On* event or the position of a pitch bend wheel in a *Pitch Bend* message.

Parts Per Quarter Note (PPQ or PPQN): The resolution of a musical device's *timebase*, based on the number of clock ticks in each quarter note. See *resolution*.

patch: The set of *parameters* for a sound stored in a *synthesizer*'s memory; also called a *program*. The word "patch" comes from the earlier synthesizers that needed patch chords in order to construct a sound.

patch bay: A device that simplifies the connecting of sources and destinations of instruments in a studio. Patch bays are available both for audio and MIDI connections.

patch editor: A computer program for creating and modifying *patches* in an instrument.

patch librarian: A computer program used to rearrange and organize the *patches* within an instrument or instruments.

PC: Personal computer.

peripheral: A device, such as a *modem* or a printer, that is added to a computer to expand the options of the system.

Pitch Bend: The act of sliding, or "bending" a note or sound by use of a wheel, slider or knob. MIDI has a code specifically for sending pitch bend messages.

Poly: A MIDI Mode that allows a synthesizer to respond polyphonically to incoming MIDI messages.

polyphonic: The performance of more than one note at a time.

Polyphonic Key Pressure: The ability of a keyboard to sense *aftertouch* on each key individually, and send MIDI messages accordingly.

port: A physical connection through which a computer transmits or receives information. MIDI uses a port with a five-pin *DIN plug*.

portamento: Sliding from one pitch to another. Many synthesizers have this capability as an option. There is a MIDI code for turning this function on and off.

PPQ: See *Parts Per Quarter Note*.

PPQN: See *Parts Per Quarter Note*.

Program Change: The MIDI code that commands an instrument to select one of its *patch* memories so it can be played.

program: In synthesis, a memory location within a *synthesizer* that holds preset sounds. Also called *patches*. In computerese, a set of instructions that tells the computer to perform a specific task.

quantize: The rounding off of rhythmic values to a particular value, such as eighth or sixteenth notes, usually used to "correct" rhythmic errors in a performance without manual editing.This is used by most sequencers and drum machines.

RAM–Random Access Memory: The type of memory that allows a *synthesizer* or computer to "read" and "write" information.

Release Velocity: The speed with which a key is released. This information is sent with a *Note Off* message.

removable media: A type of hard drive that has removable cartridges, also referred to as "removable hard disks."

resolution: The number of increments into which a clock-based device divides a unit of time such as a quarter note. Also referred to as *timebase* or *PPQ (Parts Per Quarter Note)*.

reverb: An effects device used to simulate the ambiance of a hall or room.

ROM–Read Only Memory: The kind of memory that is stored but cannot be altered.

Running Status: A technique used in many MIDI devices to reduce the number of *bytes* needed to send MIDI messages. This is accomplished by removing redundant *status bytes*.

sample: The *digital* recording of a sound. Sampling instruments have the ability to record, store, manipulate, and then play back acoustic sounds.

Sample Dump Standard: A *System Exclusive* format for MIDI *samplers* to exchange their memory with other samplers or with computers via MIDI.

sampler: A musical instrument capable of digitally recording an acoustic sound, manipulating it, and replaying it in response to MIDI messages. Each key of the keyboard will transpose the sound appropriately to produce a scale.

SCSI (Small Computer Systems Interface): A standard *interface* used by many computers to link various *peripherals* together, especially hard drives.

sequencer: In MIDI, a device that records MIDI events, similar to the way a tape recorder records sounds. Unlike tape recording, sequencers record MIDI data, not sound.

slave: A MIDI device that is controlled by another MIDI device. This can include *synthesizers* that are responding to incoming MIDI information and *drum machines* or *sequencers* set to their *MIDI sync mode*.

Smart FSK: A modified version of *FSK,* which also includes the capabilities of *Song Position Pointer*.

SMF–Standard MIDI file: A standardized format for exchanging MIDI sequences on computer disk.

SMPTE–Society of Motion Picture and Television Engineers: This technical union created the standard synchronization code for film and video.

SMPTE reader: A device able to accept and utilize incoming *SMPTE time code*.

SMPTE Time Code: A widely used synchronizing code that allows many devices to operate together. It is expressed in hours, minutes, seconds, and frames. See *MTC*.

SMPTE-to-MIDI converter: A device that reads SMPTE time code and sends *MIDI clock* messages or *MIDI Time Code*.

software: Information in the form of either data or instructions used by a hardware device: A *program* for a computer. A *sample* of a sound on a disk. Music on a record or tape. The codes inside the chips in instruments. These are all examples of software.

Song Position Pointer: The MIDI message that instructs a *drum machine* or *sequencer* to locate to a specific place in a song for playing.

Song Select: A MIDI message used to tell *sequencers* or *drum machines* which song in their memory to play.

SPP: See *Song Position Pointer*.

Start: The MIDI message sent by a master device to tell all other clock-based devices in the system to start playing from the beginning of the sequence.

status bytes: The codes that define the type of information being sent in a MIDI message. A status byte is usually followed by one or more *data bytes*, and also contains the MIDI *channel* of the event in the lower four *bits*.

Stop: The MIDI message that tells all other clock-based devices in the system to stop playing or recording.

sustain: In MIDI, a controller that causes notes to hold, even after *Note Off* commands have been received.

sync: Short for *synchronization*.

sync signal: An audio signal recorded onto tape used for the *synchronization* of clock-based devices connected in the system. See *SMPTE* and *FSK*.

sync track: The audio track on a *multitrack* recorder that contains the *sync signal*.

synchronization: The process of locking two or more machines together to play simultaneously.

synchronizers: Any device that assists in the *synchronization* of audio and video devices.

synthesizer: A musical instrument that produces sound by the use of electronic circuitry.

System Common Messages: The group of MIDI messages used primarily to enhance the functions of other commands. *Song Position Pointer, Tune Request,* and *Song Select* are System Common Messages.

System Exclusive Messages: MIDI codes for sending data for a specific instrument. These codes are often used to transfer *patch* information from one instrument to another, or to program *synthesizers* remotely through MIDI.

System Real Time Messages: MIDI messages that synchronize the performance of any clock-based MIDI devices. System Real Time messages specify *tempo, Start, Stop, Continue* and *Song Position Pointer*.

System Reset: The MIDI command that returns instruments to the condition they were in when first turned on.

tempo: The rate at which musical beats occur.

tempo maps: A list of tempo changes, sometimes found in stand alone *synchronizers* and *sequencers*.

timbre: Tone color of a sound, defined by the harmonic content of its *waveforms*.

timebase: See *resolution*.

Timing Clock: The *System Real Time* message that is used to synchronize MIDI devices together; it is sent 24 times per beat.

Tune Request: A MIDI message that commands *analog synthesizers* to retune their *oscillators*.

velocity: In MIDI, the speed with which a key, drum pad, or string is hit or released. This information is sent with all MIDI *Note On* and *Note Off* messages.

velocity sensitivity: An instrument's ability to detect and respond to *velocity*; not available in every MIDI instrument.

vibrato: A slight periodic fluctuation of pitch in a sustained note. In technical terms, it is one kind of *frequency modulation* generally occurring at rates between about three and seven times per second.

Voltage Control: The technique used by *analog synthesizers* to manipulate various sound parameters with electrical voltages.

Volume: The MIDI message used to adjust the overall output level of an instrument. There are 128 possible volume levels (0 to 127).

waveform: The shape of a sound depicted graphically as *amplitude* over time. *Oscillators* generate *waveforms*. Common waveforms in synthesis are sine, square, sawtooth, pulse and triangle.

MIDI By The Numbers

Dec	Hex	Binary		Note
0	00	0000	0000	C -1
1	01	0000	0001	C# -1
2	02	0000	0010	D -1
3	03	0000	0011	D# -1
4	04	0000	0100	E -1
5	05	0000	0101	F -1
6	06	0000	0110	F# -1
7	07	0000	0111	G -1
8	08	0000	1000	G# -1
9	09	0000	1001	A -1
10	0A	0000	1010	A# -1
11	0B	0000	1011	B -1
12	0C	0000	1100	C 0
13	0D	0000	1101	C# 0
14	0E	0000	1110	D 0
15	0F	0000	1111	D# 0
16	10	0001	0000	E 0
17	11	0001	0001	F 0
18	12	0001	0010	F# 0
19	13	0001	0011	G 0
20	14	0001	0100	G# 0
21	15	0001	0101	A 0
22	16	0001	0110	A# 0
23	17	0001	0111	B 0
24	18	0001	1000	C 1
25	19	0001	1001	C# 1
26	1A	0001	1010	D 1
27	1B	0001	1011	D# 1
28	1C	0001	1100	E 1
29	1D	0001	1101	F 1
30	1E	0001	1110	F# 1
31	1F	0001	1111	G 1
32	20	0010	0000	G# 1
33	21	0010	0001	A 1
34	22	0010	0010	A# 1
35	23	0010	0011	B 1
36	24	0010	0100	C 2
37	25	0010	0101	C# 2
38	26	0010	0110	D 2
39	27	0010	0111	D# 2
40	28	0010	1000	E 2
41	29	0010	1001	F 2
42	2A	0010	1010	F# 2
43	2B	0010	1011	G 2
44	2C	0010	1100	G# 2
45	2D	0010	1101	A 2
46	2E	0010	1110	A# 2
47	2F	0010	1111	B 2
48	30	0011	0000	C 3
49	31	0011	0001	C# 3
50	32	0011	0010	D 3
51	33	0011	0011	D# 3
52	34	0011	0100	E 3
53	35	0011	0101	F 3
54	36	0011	0110	F# 3
55	37	0011	0111	G 3
56	38	0011	1000	G# 3
57	39	0011	1001	A 3
58	3A	0011	1010	A# 3
59	3B	0011	1011	B 3
60	3C	0011	1100	C 4
61	3D	0011	1101	C# 4
62	3E	0011	1110	D 4
63	3F	0011	1111	D# 4

Dec	Hex	Binary		Note
64	40	0100	0000	E 4
65	41	0100	0001	F 4
66	42	0100	0010	F# 4
67	43	0100	0011	G 4
68	44	0100	0100	G# 4
69	45	0100	0101	A 4
70	46	0100	0110	A# 4
71	47	0100	0111	B 4
72	48	0100	1000	C 5
73	49	0100	1001	C# 5
74	4A	0100	1010	D 5
75	4B	0100	1011	D# 5
76	4C	0100	1100	E 5
77	4D	0100	1101	F 5
78	4E	0100	1110	F# 5
79	4F	0100	1111	G 5
80	50	0101	0000	G# 5
81	51	0101	0001	A 5
82	52	0101	0010	A# 5
83	53	0101	0011	B 5
84	54	0101	0100	C 6
85	55	0101	0101	C# 6
86	56	0101	0110	D 6
87	57	0101	0111	D# 6
88	58	0101	1000	E 6
89	59	0101	1001	F 6
90	5A	0101	1010	F# 6
91	5B	0101	1011	G 6
92	5C	0101	1100	G# 6
93	5D	0101	1101	A 6
94	5E	0101	1110	A# 6
95	5F	0101	1111	B 6
96	60	0110	0000	C 7
97	61	0110	0001	C# 7
98	62	0110	0010	D 7
99	63	0110	0011	D# 7
100	64	0110	0100	E 7
101	65	0110	0101	F 7
102	66	0110	0110	F# 7
103	67	0110	0111	G 7
104	68	0110	1000	G# 7
105	69	0110	1001	A 7
106	6A	0110	1010	A# 7
107	6B	0110	1011	B 7
108	6C	0110	1100	C 8
109	6D	0110	1101	C# 8
110	6E	0110	1110	D 8
111	6F	0110	1111	D# 8
112	70	0111	0000	E 8
113	71	0111	0001	F 8
114	72	0111	0010	F# 8
115	73	0111	0011	G 8
116	74	0111	0100	G# 8
117	75	0111	0101	A 8
118	76	0111	0110	A# 8
119	77	0111	0111	B 8
120	78	0111	1000	C 9
121	79	0111	1001	C# 9
122	7A	0111	1010	D 9
123	7B	0111	1011	D# 9
124	7C	0111	1100	E 9
125	7D	0111	1101	F 9
126	7E	0111	1110	F# 9
127	7F	0111	1111	G 9

Dec	Hex	Binary		Message	Channel
128	80	1000	0000	Note Off	Chan. 1
129	81	1000	0001	Note Off	Chan. 2
130	82	1000	0010	Note Off	Chan. 3
131	83	1000	0011	Note Off	Chan. 4
132	84	1000	0100	Note Off	Chan. 5
133	85	1000	0101	Note Off	Chan. 6
134	86	1000	0110	Note Off	Chan. 7
135	87	1000	0111	Note Off	Chan. 8
136	88	1000	1000	Note Off	Chan. 9
137	89	1000	1001	Note Off	Chan. 10
138	8A	1000	1010	Note Off	Chan. 11
139	8B	1000	1011	Note Off	Chan. 12
140	8C	1000	1100	Note Off	Chan. 13
141	8D	1000	1101	Note Off	Chan. 14
142	8E	1000	1110	Note Off	Chan. 15
143	8F	1000	1111	Note Off	Chan. 16
144	90	1001	0000	Note On	Chan. 1
145	91	1001	0001	Note On	Chan. 2
146	92	1001	0010	Note On	Chan. 3
147	93	1001	0011	Note On	Chan. 4
148	94	1001	0100	Note On	Chan. 5
149	95	1001	0101	Note On	Chan. 6
150	96	1001	0110	Note On	Chan. 7
151	97	1001	0111	Note On	Chan. 8
152	98	1001	1000	Note On	Chan. 9
153	99	1001	1001	Note On	Chan. 10
154	9A	1001	1010	Note On	Chan. 11
155	9B	1001	1011	Note On	Chan. 12
156	9C	1001	1100	Note On	Chan. 13
157	9D	1001	1101	Note On	Chan. 14
158	9E	1001	1110	Note On	Chan. 15
159	9F	1001	1111	Note On	Chan. 16
160	A0	1010	0000	PK Pressure	Chan. 1
161	A1	1010	0001	PK Pressure	Chan. 2
162	A2	1010	0010	PK Pressure	Chan. 3
163	A3	1010	0011	PK Pressure	Chan. 4
164	A4	1010	0100	PK Pressure	Chan. 5
165	A5	1010	0101	PK Pressure	Chan. 6
166	A6	1010	0110	PK Pressure	Chan. 7
167	A7	1010	0111	PK Pressure	Chan. 8
168	A8	1010	1000	PK Pressure	Chan. 9
169	A9	1010	1001	PK Pressure	Chan. 10
170	AA	1010	1010	PK Pressure	Chan. 11
171	AB	1010	1011	PK Pressure	Chan. 12
172	AC	1010	1100	PK Pressure	Chan. 13
173	AD	1010	1101	PK Pressure	Chan. 14
174	AE	1010	1110	PK Pressure	Chan. 15
175	AF	1010	1111	PK Pressure	Chan. 16
176	B0	1011	0000	Control Chng	Chan. 1
177	B1	1011	0001	Control Chng	Chan. 2
178	B2	1011	0010	Control Chng	Chan. 3
179	B3	1011	0011	Control Chng	Chan. 4
180	B4	1011	0100	Control Chng	Chan. 5
181	B5	1011	0101	Control Chng	Chan. 6
182	B6	1011	0110	Control Chng	Chan. 7
183	B7	1011	0111	Control Chng	Chan. 8
184	B8	1011	1000	Control Chng	Chan. 9
185	B9	1011	1001	Control Chng	Chan. 10
186	BA	1011	1010	Control Chng	Chan. 11
187	BB	1011	1011	Control Chng	Chan. 12
188	BC	1011	1100	Control Chng	Chan. 13
189	BD	1011	1101	Control Chng	Chan. 14
190	BE	1011	1110	Control Chng	Chan. 15
191	BF	1011	1111	Control Chng	Chan. 16

Dec	Hex	Binary		Message	Channel
192	C0	1100	0000	Program Chng	Chan. 1
193	C1	1100	0001	Program Chng	Chan. 2
194	C2	1100	0010	Program Chng	Chan. 3
195	C3	1100	0011	Program Chng	Chan. 4
196	C4	1100	0100	Program Chng	Chan. 5
197	C5	1100	0101	Program Chng	Chan. 6
198	C6	1100	0110	Program Chng	Chan. 7
199	C7	1100	0111	Program Chng	Chan. 8
200	C8	1100	1000	Program Chng	Chan. 9
201	C9	1100	1001	Program Chng	Chan. 10
202	CA	1100	1010	Program Chng	Chan. 11
203	CB	1100	1011	Program Chng	Chan. 12
204	CC	1100	1100	Program Chng	Chan. 13
205	CD	1100	1101	Program Chng	Chan. 14
206	CE	1100	1110	Program Chng	Chan. 15
207	CF	1100	1111	Program Chng	Chan. 16
208	D0	1101	0000	Channel Pres	Chan. 1
209	D1	1101	0001	Channel Pres	Chan. 2
210	D2	1101	0010	Channel Pres	Chan. 3
211	D3	1101	0011	Channel Pres	Chan. 4
212	D4	1101	0100	Channel Pres	Chan. 5
213	D5	1101	0101	Channel Pres	Chan. 6
214	D6	1101	0110	Channel Pres	Chan. 7
215	D7	1101	0111	Channel Pres	Chan. 8
216	D8	1101	1000	Channel Pres	Chan. 9
217	D9	1101	1001	Channel Pres	Chan. 10
218	DA	1101	1010	Channel Pres	Chan. 11
219	DB	1101	1011	Channel Pres	Chan. 12
220	DC	1101	1100	Channel Pres	Chan. 13
221	DD	1101	1101	Channel Pres	Chan. 14
222	DE	1101	1110	Channel Pres	Chan. 15
223	DF	1101	1111	Channel Pres	Chan. 16
224	E0	1110	0000	Pitch Bend Ch	Chan. 1
225	E1	1110	0001	Pitch Bend Ch	Chan. 2
226	E2	1110	0010	Pitch Bend Ch	Chan. 3
227	E3	1110	0011	Pitch Bend Ch	Chan. 4
228	E4	1110	0100	Pitch Bend Ch	Chan. 5
229	E5	1110	0101	Pitch Bend Ch	Chan. 6
230	E6	1110	0110	Pitch Bend Ch	Chan. 7
231	E7	1110	0111	Pitch Bend Ch	Chan. 8
232	E8	1110	1000	Pitch Bend Ch	Chan. 9
233	E9	1110	1001	Pitch Bend Ch	Chan. 10
234	EA	1110	1010	Pitch Bend Ch	Chan. 11
235	EB	1110	1011	Pitch Bend Ch	Chan. 12
236	EC	1110	1100	Pitch Bend Ch	Chan. 13
237	ED	1110	1101	Pitch Bend Ch	Chan. 14
238	EE	1110	1110	Pitch Bend Ch	Chan. 15
239	EF	1110	1111	Pitch Bend Ch	Chan. 16
240	F0	1111	0000	System Exclusive	
241	F1	1111	0001	MIDI Time Code	
242	F2	1111	0010	Song Position Pointer	
243	F3	1111	0011	Song Select	
244	F4	1111	0100	Undefined	
245	F5	1111	0101	Undefined	
246	F6	1111	0110	Tune Request	
247	F7	1111	0111	End OF Exclusive	
248	F8	1111	1000	Timing Clock	
249	F9	1111	1001	Undefined	
250	FA	1111	1010	Start	
251	FB	1111	1011	Stop	
252	FC	1111	1100	Continue	
253	FD	1111	1101	Undefined	
254	FE	1111	1110	Active Sensing	
255	FF	1111	1111	System Reset	

THANKS

The author wishes to thank those people who helped me during the writing of this book. I wish to firstly thank Jim Mothersbaugh, Tadao Sakai and Richard King for showing me this thing called MIDI. Thanks to Chris Meyer for pointing out the occasional folly of my ways, and for understanding or thinking up all this stuff in the first place. Thanks to Jim Cooper for adding so greatly to my knowledge and to my phone bill. Thanks to Lachlan Westfall of the International MIDI Association for keeping it all together and coming my way.

Thanks go to Ronny Schiff, my editor. If you can understand this, or any other sentence in this book, it is because of her. Thanks to Jaynee Thorne and Mollie Gordon for reading and rereading this book until it made some sense. Thanks to Rich Leeds and Jim Mona for additional photos, and to Perry Leopold of the PAN Network for bringing so many people so close together. Thanks to Kevin Laubach for his assistance.

Very special thanks to my friend Scott Wilkinson for the generous looks over both my shoulders, and for the courage to ask the question "What exactly do you mean here?" Thanks to Judy Silk for her encouragement, patience and Isak.

And of course, thanks Mom.

Jeff Rona is a composer and arranger for film, television, and theater, as well as a synthesist and musician in Los Angeles. He is a reformed software developer who spent four years creating computer-based sequencers. He is the coordinator of the Electronic Music Program for UCLA Extension and is a columnist for Keyboard Magazine. He was a founder and a past president of the MIDI Manufacturers Association, the international consortium of MIDI hardware and software makers.

He can be reached on the Internet at "jrona@pan.com", or on the PAN network at "jrona".

FOR MORE INFORMATION

MIDI is changing, expanding, and adapting to new musical needs all the time. To stay aware of current events in the world of MIDI, it is worth your consideration to subscribe to any of the current electronic music periodicals.

For those interested in becoming more involved in music or audio for film and video, you may wish to look at my book *Synchronization From Reel To Reel*, also available from Hal Leonard Books. It is a thorough description of using time code and related devices for home or professional studio applications.

The largest MIDI users group in the world is the International MIDI Association (IMA). They provide up-to-date information on MIDI hardware and software through their newsletter and phone hotline. They are also the distributors of the official *MIDI Detailed Specification* written by the MIDI Manufacturers Association, as well as several additional technical documents on MIDI. These are especially important to anyone interested in designing MIDI software or hardware. Readers of *The MIDI Companion* receive a discount on membership to the IMA by mentioning the name of this book. Membership information can be requested by writing to the following address:

The International MIDI Association
23643 Emelita Street
Woodland Hills, CA 91367 USA
(818) 598-0088

SOME PUBLICATIONS OF INTEREST

Electronic Musician Magazine
6400 Hollis Street #12
Emeryville, CA 94608
(415) 653-3307

Keyboard Magazine
411 Borel Ave., Suite 100
San Mateo, CA 94402
(415) 358-9500

EQ Magazine
PSN Publications
2 Park Ave. Suite 1820
New York, NY 10016
(212) 213-3444

PERFORMING ARTISTS NETWORK (PAN)

One of the revolutionary aspects of working as an electronic musician today is the ability to communicate with other artists and technicians via computer. With an inexpensive modem, you can be in contact with a large number of people with a vast array of information and skills. Established in 1987, the PAN Network is the oldest and largest MUSIC network serving professionals in ALL aspects of the music business. While some other computer networks have jumped on the MIDI bandwagon in recent years, the PAN Network has remained dedicated to just one thing and one thing only—MUSIC! Among its many many benefits, PAN features:

- Thousands of members, all professionals, from over 40 countries worldwide

- Thousands of downloadable files

- Direct Hotlines to over 225 music and audio-related companies

- Free software to completely AUTOMATE your usage.

- Free Classified Ads.

- Online Job Center

- Online Entertainment Law Center

- Local access worldwide (over 900 cities) via Tymnet, Telenet, and Internet.

- Dozens of Special Interest Groups and Bulletin Boards

- UseNet archives, Internet gateways, and FTP transfers.

- The most sophisticated and least expensive FAX services in the world.

- Travel Services with the lowest airfares, guaranteed.

- Optional delivery of the entire network on DISK each month.

- Optional auto-forwarding of messages directly to your FAX machine, instantly.

- Connect-Free conferences and "Free Zones" each month.

- Connect-Free MONTHS for people who upload files or recruit new members.

PAN Membership costs a one-time signup fee of $225, but for buyer's of *The MIDI Companion*, the signup fee is discounted to only $25 through December 31, 1995. There is also a low hourly fee for using PAN, which is explained during your initial on-line session.

ONLINE SIGNUP PROCEDURES

PAN can be reached by a local call from over 900 U.S. cities and 75 foreign countries, via Telenet, Tymnet, or Internet. To sign up, please do the following:

1. Dial your local access number. If you do not know the Tymnet or Telenet numbers in your area, you may contact customer service for Tymnet at (800) 336-0149 or Telenet at (800) 877-5045. You may also dial-in directly to 617-576-0862. Members in Europe and Australasia should obtain an NUI from your country's Postal, Telephone & Telegraph (PTT) office.

2. Depending whether you call in through Tymnet, Telenet, Direct, Internet,or Overseas, do the following:

> Direct: <CR> <CR> (that is: two RETURNs)

> Internet: telnet pan.com

> Telenet: <CR> <CR> <CR> (that is: three RETURN's)
> Then at the @ prompt, type C PAN
> (Note: if dialing in at 2400 baud, type "@D" when you first connect)

> Tymnet: Type the letter "O" (without the quotes)
> Then at the "Please Login:" prompt, type PAN

Overseas: PAN's International Host ID number is: 311061703093. If for any reason that number will not connect, our back up Host number is: 310661703088. Note that some countries, this number may be preceeded or followed by a zero. Please consult your local PT&T for more details.

3. In all cases, at "Username:" type: PANJOIN

4. At "Password:" type: RONABOOK

You will then be welcomed to PAN's Online Signup area, and prompted for all billing information needed to set up your PAN account. During the signup you will also be asked to choose a "Username" and will be given a temporary "Password."

If you have any questions, or require further information, please contact PAN at (215) 584-0300, or write P.O. Box 162, Skippack, PA 19474 U.S.A., or FAX: 215-584-1038

INDEX